BE STILL
AND
LISTEN

William McDonald

Book Design by Aeyshaa

Cover Illustrator by Laird Atkins

ISBN #979-8-9872043-1-3

TABLE OF CONTENTS

CHAPTER I

Maggie was showering when the feeling first came over her. Even with the hot water pouring on her, a cold shiver ran along her spine and a gnawing thought entered her mind: *she shouldn't take the bus to school today.*

She tried to dismiss this strange idea. She really enjoyed her time on the bus, seeing and talking to her friends before she had to begin thinking about her classes and focusing on the day. Still, No matter how many times she pushed away the thought. The idea that she shouldn't take the bus kept creeping back in.

As she finished drying off, fixing her hair and getting dressed, she wondered what her mom might think of her wanting a ride to school instead of taking the bus. "Oh well," she said to herself, "I guess I'll just have to ask her to find out." She headed to the kitchen where she knew her mom was making breakfast. She could even smell the bacon frying.

As soon as she entered the kitchen, Maggie said, "Mom, I need a favor."

Her mom turned to her and asked, "OK, how much do you need this time?"

Maggie replied, "Nothing, not this time. I know it's out of your way, but would you please give me a ride to school this morning?"

"Why not take the bus as usual, sweetheart? You're always telling me how much you enjoy taking the bus and talking to all your friends before the school day starts."

"I don't know. All I know is that while I was taking my shower, I got this strange feeling not to take the bus today," answered Maggie.

"No problem honey. I don't mind dropping you off on the way to my work, we just need to leave a little earlier so I don't end up late for work."

Maggie's body immediately relaxed and she let out a small sigh of relief.

* * *

As her mother pulled up to the front of the school, Maggie noticed Gabe getting out of the car in front of them. *How odd. Why did he get a ride to school,* she thought. They normally sat together on the bus and talked all the way to school and back home again in the afternoon. Instead, it looked like Gabe's dad drove him to school today.

Maggie's mom waved to Mr. Hidalgo, Gabe's dad. He gestured to her and mouthed the word, "Hello." Since both parents had to get to work, Maggie's mom followed Gabe's dad as they, along with other cars pulled away from the curb and headed out to Main Street.

Gabe headed toward her with a puzzled look on his face as if surprised to see her being dropped off by her mom. "Why didn't you take the bus?" he asked as soon as he was in hearing distance.

"It's really weird," Maggie said. "I got this eerie feeling during my shower this morning and just knew I wasn't supposed to take the bus today."

"Wow," replied Gabe. "I had this gut feeling, during breakfast, to ask my dad to bring me this morning and not to take the bus."

A little frown furrowed Gabe's forehead, but his deep brown eyes still shone with that genuine kindness that was so familiar to her. She had a hard time pulling her gaze away from those eyes of his, but she did.

Just as she turned to look away from Gabe, she spotted her friend Rose running up to them. At that very moment, the same strange shiver she had felt in the shower ran up Maggie's spine.

Rose was slightly out of breath by the time she reached the two of them, but was able to blurt out, "I just heard about the bus crash. Are the two of you OK? What I heard was that it was your bus that crashed."

Looking totally confused and noticing Gabe had a puzzled look too, Maggie turned to Rose and said, "What are you talking about? What bus crash? Who said it was our bus?"

"Yeah," Gabe said, with a sense of urgency in his voice. "What bus crash? We haven't heard anything, and neither of us were on the bus this morning. Our parents drove us."

Looking even more bewildered, Rose answered, "One of the tires on bus 1206 blew out, and the bus ran off the road and flipped on its side. The words I heard were that some of the kids got hurt badly and that police and ambulances were taking them to the hospital. They say some only got a couple of cuts and scratches that required stitches, but some had their arms and legs in braces. That's all I've heard. I figured you guys were on the bus because you take that bus every day to and from school."

Maggie was still feeling shaken by the news, and she could see, by the look on Gabe's face, that he felt the same way. Just then the bell rang for homeroom so she didn't have time to say anything to Gabe.

As they headed into school, Gabe turned to Maggie and said, "We definitely need to talk about all this. I'll see you in the cafeteria at lunch."

"Sure," Maggie said, still stunned by the strange turn of events.

Sitting in homeroom, Maggie could not shake that agitated feeling as her teacher started taking attendance and began roll call, in alphabetical order. It always seemed to take forever to get to her since her last name was Woodbridge. Before her teacher got halfway through the alphabet, Principal Preston's voice came over the loudspeaker, telling the entire school about what happened to bus 1206. His account of the accident was almost the same as Rose's but in more detail. She learned that her driver, Mike, had been knocked out of his seat and hit the door when the bus flipped on its side. The principal said his seat belt saved him from going through the front windshield. The principal added that some of the students were being released from the hospital after their cuts were stitched up. The ones who suffered more trauma would likely stay at least overnight.

Maggie felt a wave of nausea rise in her as she thought about her other friends on that bus. *Which ones were safe and relatively unharmed and which ones were more seriously injured?* Her thoughts raced in a thousand different directions at the same time.

"For those of you who normally ride bus 1206 but were not on the bus this morning, we are making other arrangements for you to get home this afternoon. If you normally take bus 1206, please stop by the main office and let my staff know so they can arrange for your transportation home. We are also making preparations for a different bus to run the route tomorrow for you to get to and from school. If we get any additional information on the students involved and the seriousness of their injuries, I will make another announcement. Thank you."

The beacon and eggs she had gulped down in time to leave home early remained unsettled in Maggie's stomach. All she could do was wonder about her friends, but there was something else. Why had she been spared this accident? What led her to ask her mother for a ride? She hardly knew what to make of this series of events. She felt thankful she didn't take the bus, yet she was equally worried about those who did. First, second, and third periods passed without much focus. She remained in her inner world, waffling back and forth between worrying about her friends on the bus and wondering about that cold shiver and the unnerving sense of inner knowing she had experienced. By the time lunch arrived, she had totally tuned out of her three classes and felt as if her skin were crawling.

* * *

As the last class before lunch ended, all Gabe could think about was talking to Maggie, finding out more about their friends, and figuring out his gut feeling that morning that had led him to ask his father for a ride and not take the school bus.

As he entered the cafeteria, he saw Maggie waving her arm to get his attention. She never had to do anything to draw his attention though. He thought of her often, and her presence always prompted a smile, even though he tried to hide his excitement at seeing her every day. He pointed to the food line so he could get his lunch first.

After he filled his tray, he headed over to the table where Maggie had saved him a seat.

As he sat down, he said, "I couldn't concentrate on any of my classes this morning. All I could think about was what happened to the bus and how we both ended up not getting on it this morning."

Before he could say anything else, the principal came back on the PA system. "The staff and I were just informed that most of your classmates and the driver have been released from the hospital and taken home. Many of them had severe cuts from flying glass and required stitches. Those who are being kept overnight have broken bones that require resetting, but the doctors say they will be fine. The doctors just want to make sure there are no further complications. Those students will be released tomorrow, barring any additional problems. My staff and I ask all of you to please keep all of them in your prayers."

After the announcement ended, Gabe looked into Maggie's clear blue eyes and wondered what she was thinking about all this.

"Gabe, it's so weird," she said. "I still don't understand why the thought came to me about not taking the bus. And that you had that same kind of feeling. Thank goodness everyone is OK."

With food still in his mouth, Gabe replied, "Yeah, I was thinking the same thing all morning. You know, I have had feelings like this before but never like this one. How about you?"

Not being able to look directly at him, Maggie answered, "Yeah, once or twice. I remember once thinking about calling one of my girlfriends and at that very moment my phone rang and it was her. Some of my friends have told me things like that have happened to them too. With all that's going on, I think I need to talk to my mom tonight about all this, both the bus accident and why I had that feeling about not taking the bus. This morning was just way too weird not to talk about it. Maybe she knows something I don't."

Although he was distracted by his thoughts about their strange feelings, Gabe heard Maggie's idea about discussing it with her mother. "Maybe you could mention that I had a gut feeling not to take the bus too. I'd be interested in what your mom has to say about it."

* * *

When the last bell rang, Gabe and Maggie headed to the main office for their ride home. As they waited, they realized they were the only two who did not take the bus that morning, so it was easy for one of the secretaries to drive them home.

As they approached Maggie's home, Gabe turned and said, "I never realized we lived so close to each other. I only live about seven blocks away from here over on Holly Farm Road."

"Gabe, you know I know where you live," Maggie said, "since I get on the bus before your house; But I forgot you didn't know where I live."

Gabe put his hand to his forehead in a gesture that said he should have realized that.

"Since we live so close, I guess we should get together some weekend," Maggie added as she was getting out of the car.

"Sounds good to me," he shouted as the car door was closing. "See you tomorrow and don't forget to talk to your mom."

Turning back, she smiled and nodded her head, indicating she heard him and wouldn't forget.

* * *

As they sat down at the dinner table, Maggie's kid brother asked if she knew any of the kids on the bus that crashed that morning.

"What crash?" Their mom asked, dropping her fork, and looking totally panicked.

Even her dad stopped eating when Josh asked about the crash. "I haven't heard anything about a crash this morning. Did you dear?"

"No, this is the first I have heard about any crash. What happened? Was anyone hurt?" asked her dad.

Maggie put down her fork. With her elbows on the table and her hands folded, she began to tell her parents about the crash that happened to the bus she took every morning. She explained about the blown tire and the bus running off the road and overturning. She described the injuries and condition of the other students and the bus driver based on what the principal said. She added that both she and her friend Gabe were the only two who did not take the bus.

Looking a little confused, her mom asked, "Is that why you wanted me to take you to school this morning? I remember you saying something about some kind of feeling that you shouldn't take the bus."

"Yes, Mom. And what's even stranger is that my friend Gabe had what he called a gut feeling not to take the bus, which is why his dad drove him. That's what I was hoping to talk to you about, why we had these feelings not to take the bus," she said.

"I'm Sorry honey, but your dad and I have a meeting tonight and you need to watch Josh. I would be more than happy to talk to you about all this some other time, but I can't tonight. How about we set aside some time this weekend to talk about it," replied her mom.

Looking a little down, Maggie responded, "Thanks anyway Mom. Maybe I'll go to my room and see if I can find anything on YouTube or text one of my friends to see if they might know something."

Talking with his mouth full of food, Josh jumped in, "I get those kinds of feelings a lot but never paid much attention to them."

No now responded to Josh. They all went back to finishing their dinners and having dessert.

After cleaning up the table, Maggie loaded and ran the dishwasher and then checked on Josh. He was busy with his video games, so she headed to her room to see what she could find out on the internet. While reading an article about intuition, her phone rang with a video call from her friend Michelle, who attended a different high school.

"Hey, girl! What's up?" asked Michelle. "Anything interesting going on in your world? My mom said she saw on the news about a school bus that had blown a tire, run off the road, and flipped on its side. Have you heard about it?"

"Heard about it? It was my bus that I take every day," said Maggie.

Looking shocked, Michelle yelled, "What? Why didn't you me? Did you get hurt? Did anyone die? So, tell me. What happened?"

"Slow down girl," Maggie yelled back. "I'll tell you everything I know. First off, I was not on the bus. Something told me not to take the bus this morning, so my mom drove me. As you heard, the bus blew a tire ran off the road, and flipped on its side. The driver and kids on the bus were taken to the hospital with cuts and broken bones. Many of them had to have stitches to have their bones reset. Some of them had to stay overnight just to make sure everything was OK, but the others were sent home with their parents by lunchtime. Me and one other kid, Gabe, were the only two not on the bus. Gabe said that he had a gut feeling not to take the bus, so his dad drove him. End of story."

"OK, wait a minute. Is this the same Gabe you've talked about in the past?

The boy you said you like but never told him?" asked Michelle.

Smiling like a little kid, Maggie said, "Yeah, that's him, but he still doesn't know that I like him. All he knows is that we talk every day on the bus to and from school and sometimes at lunch. We rode home together with one of the secretaries this afternoon. It was the first time he had seen how close I live to him."

"Wow. What luck you have girl! Sometimes I wish I had your luck," Michelle said, giggling.

The two of them chatted for ages, and before they both knew it, it was almost 10 pm.

Looking at her clock, Michelle said, "Did you know we have been talking for over two and a half hours? I still have some homework to finish."

"Oh hell, so do I," said Maggie. "I'll call tomorrow night after dinner to let you know how things went with Gabe tomorrow. He said we would talk again at lunch."

"OK, you lucky girl. Wish I knew someone like Gabe at my school. Good night girlfriend."

Maggie had forgotten about checking all her social media pages but turned off her phone anyway. She had to get her homework done and get to bed at a, somewhat, reasonable hour.

Looking at her clock, as she was climbing into bed, Maggie saw that it was about 10:53. *Not bad. I was able to get all my homework done in less than an hour,* she thought to herself.

She was so tired that she was falling asleep even before her head hit the pillow.

At some point during the night, she began dreaming about the bus accident. Her dream was so real it felt like she was there. As the crash happened in the dream, she woke up feeling shaken. *Why was I dreaming about being on the bus when I wasn't even there,* she thought. *Maybe the dream was letting me know what it would have been like if I had been on the bus.* Not wanting to think about it any longer, she lay back down and fell asleep again. The dream continued where it left off. She was being taken to the hospital in an ambulance. She could feel the pain from the cuts beneath the quake and tape. A flash of flying glass popped into her mind as she looked at her injuries. As she looked down, she saw that her right leg was in a splint. The sound of the siren started to fade as they pulled into the hospital, and she was taken into the Emergency Room. A doctor came in and said something about surgery to a nurse. She couldn't understand what he was saying. Then she saw her parents run into the area where she was. They looked very upset and her mom was crying.

"Sweetheart, are you OK? Dad and I were so worried when we got the call," her mom said, fighting back the tears.

The doctor turned to her parents and told them about her right leg being broken in numerous places. They said she needed surgery to put in a metal rod below the knee. Her parents looked so worried as they wheeled her away into the operating room.

Just then, Maggie's alarm clock went off and she jumped out of bed, as if in shock.

What was that all about? Again she wondered if this dream was showing her what would have happened if she had been on the bus.

Not wanting to think any more about the dream, she got up, showered, and dressed for school.

On the way downstairs for breakfast, she wondered if she should ask her mom about her dream but decided it would be best not to say anything.

CHAPTER II

After breakfast, Maggie grabbed her coat and backpack and headed to the bus stop.

The bus arrived about five minutes late but, to her surprise, her normal driver was seated behind the wheel. She could see his left arm covered in a bandage.

"Wow, I didn't expect to see you driving us this morning after what happened to you yesterday," she said as she entered the bus. "I thought you would be off today recuperating,"

"No, I felt it was important for all you kids to see me today and know that I am OK and that it was just a freak thing yesterday. I found out it was a faulty tire that caused the blowout. All the buses are checked over each day after the last run, and that bus checked out fine. So, it was decided that it was just a freak thing and probably wouldn't happen again in a million years," said Mike, the driver. "Once I pick up the last of you kids, I'll fully explain what happened."

A couple of stops later, Gabe got on and took a seat next to Maggie.

"Can you believe Mike is back behind the wheel this morning?" Gabe asked.

"Good morning to you too, Gabe," Maggie said sarcastically. "I was surprised too, but he said he would stop the bus and tell everyone what happened yesterday and why, so let's just wait to see what he says."

* * *

Right after the last pickup, Mike stopped the bus and explained that yesterday's crash was a freak accident caused when a tire blew. He said that the records for bus 1206 showed that the tire was new and had just been installed the previous Thursday night.

"I was lucky," Mike said. "All I got were some deep cuts that required stitches, nothing else." With that, he got back behind the wheel and drove to the school.

* * *

After they arrived and everyone got off the bus, Maggie turned to Gabe and said, "I don't have time now, but at lunch, I'll tell you all about this dream I had last night."

"Tell me now," replied Gabe. "We still have a few minutes before the bell rings. Did you get to talk to your mom about your strange feeling and my gut feeling?"

"No, and too much to tell you. You'll just have to wait until lunch." Maggie replied as she headed off to her homeroom.

During homeroom, the PA sounded, and Principal Preston's voice came on.

"I was just informed by the hospital that those students who remained overnight will be released this morning. There were no further complications with any of them. The staff and I want to let the entire student body know that we have special counselors in the auditorium today and tomorrow for anyone who feels they need to talk about what happened yesterday with bus 1206. These counselors will be available all day and this afternoon after school. I'll

26

make sure they are also available all day tomorrow. No need to schedule a time; just walk in and talk to any of the counselors."

Maggie felt glad she hadn't been on the bus the day before and thankful that those who were involved in the accident would have a chance to talk with someone if they needed to. She still wondered at the fact that she and Gabe experienced those strange feelings that led them to get rides with their parents. The dream from last night played in her mind, but she needed to focus open what was happening in class today, so she tried to bring herself back to the present.

* * *

Gabe gazed at the clock over and over throughout the morning. *These classes seem to last forever. Are we ever going to get to lunch?* He thought.

Finally, the bell rang, ending his last class before lunch. He was in such a hurry to get to lunch to hear all that Maggie had to tell him, that he almost knocked over a couple of kids on the way to the cafeteria.

He rushed so much that he made it through the line and sat down at the table just as Maggie was getting into line to get her food.

Gabe didn't wait until she sat down before he excitedly said. "So, tell me what your mom said and then you can tell me about your dream if we have time."

Once Maggie sat down and started eating, she looked at Gabe and said, "I didn't get a chance to talk to my mom last night. She and Dad had a meeting to go to and she didn't have the time to talk. All we talked about at dinner was about the accident and how lucky I was that I wasn't on the bus. I even told her about your gut feeling and that you didn't take the bus either. After dinner, I went up to my room to check out the internet about these feelings but didn't get a chance. Michelle called and we were on the phone for a couple of hours. I did tell her about my strange feelings yesterday, and she said she has had feelings like that at times too. In fact, during dinner, when I told my parents about my gut feeling, my little brother said he has had gut feelings too, but most of the time he ignores them. Anyway, by the time Michelle and I got off the phone, it was so late, and I had to do my homework."

Looking puzzled, Gabe asked, "So what about this dream of yours? What was it all about? Was I in it?"

"If you were, I didn't see you," Maggie said. She then went on, to explain the entire dream to Gabe, including the part about going into surgery to have a metal rod put in her right leg.

"Did the surgery hurt? How did it feel having that metal rod in your leg?" asked Gabe.

"I don't know. The last thing I remembered was being wheeled into the operating room. At that point, my alarm went off and I had to get up," answered Maggie. "I want to talk to my mom tonight about all of it, the dream and the strange feeling."

"Wow. Do you think the dream was about what would have happened to you if you had been on the bus yesterday?" Gabe asked.

"I don't know, but that makes sense," she replied. "Think maybe I should go to talk to one of the counselors this afternoon? My science teacher said that the teachers were told that if any of their students wanted to go see a counselor this afternoon, they should allow them to go and not ask any questions. I think I am going to tell my social studies teacher I want to go talk to one of the counselors. What do you think?"

Gabe just sat there for a minute considering and then said, "I think that's a good idea. I was thinking about my gut feeling all last night but didn't want to say anything to my parents. I thought they might have said it was something dumb and to forget about it. Do you think I should go talk to a counselor too?"

"It wouldn't hurt. What could they say? They might be able to help both of us." Maggie said.

They didn't realize that they talked all through lunch as the bell rang for their next class.

Turning back to Maggie, Gabe yelled, "See you after school at the bus."

Maggie just waved back as if to say OK.

* * *

When Maggie got to her social studies class, she told her teacher, Miss Applegate, that she wanted to go talk to one of the counselors.

Miss Applegate didn't question her at all. She just nodded, giving permission.

When Maggie got to the auditorium, she saw about 15 different counselors, a few men, and the rest women.

She decided to go to the woman in the back of the auditorium thinking it might be better if no one else heard what she was going to discuss.

"Hi, My name is Angela Kennedy. How can I help you? Is this about the bus accident yesterday?" There woman asked.

Looking a little nervous, Maggie said, "Yes and no. It is about the accident but also about something that happened yesterday morning when I was showering and again last night in one of my dreams."

"Please sit down and tell me all about your concerns," Mrs. Kennedy said.

Maggie began her story. "Yesterday morning, when I was showering and getting ready for school, I had this strange feeling that I should not take the bus. I told my mom and she said she would take me." Maggie went on and told her story to Mrs. Kennedy, even including the fact that Gabe had a gut feeling not to take the bus.

"Gabe and I both didn't know what these feelings were all about. I was going to talk to my mom last night, but she and my dad had a meeting to go to. I did talk to a friend of mine, Michelle, who said she has had those kinds of feelings in the past too. My little brother even said he has had gut feelings but ignored them." Maggie then went on to tell Mrs. Kennedy all about her dream of being on the bus and getting severely injured.

"Let me say that I too have had these so-called strange or gut feelings," replied Mrs. Kennedy. "I don't know much about them. I do have a very good friend who, I believe, knows all about these things. I'll contact her this evening and have her come to the school with me tomorrow so you can tell her your story. I am sure she will be able to help you and maybe even Gabe. Do you think he might be willing to come tomorrow too?"

"I'm sure he would be," Maggie answered. "Oh, there he is now," she added seeing Gabe walk in. "Let me go get him and see if he will come to tomorrow." With that, Maggie went to get Gabe. Bringing him back to where Mrs. Kennedy was, she introduced them.

"Yes, I would like to come tomorrow and see what your friend can tell us. This gut feeling I had was not the first time, but it was never as strong as this one was," stated Gabe.

"Great, why don't we plan on meeting this same time tomorrow, right after your lunch," commented Mrs. Kennedy. "Now, why don't you two head back to class I'll see you tomorrow."

So Gabe and Maggie returned to their respective classes.

Before too long, the bell rang ending class for the day.

* * *

"Hey Maggie, thanks for including me in your talk with Mrs. Kennedy. When I went to the auditorium, I had no idea what I was going to say or who I should even talk to," Gabe said as they stepped onto the bus. Again, sitting next to each other, Maggie turned to Gabe, "I just knew you wanted to know more about your gut feeling, so after I told Mrs. Kennedy all about my feelings and my dream, I told her you had a feeling too and didn't know what it was all about. That's when you walked into the auditorium. Mrs. Kennedy had asked me if you would be interested in coming tomorrow too. That's when I saw you and went to get you. Why did you come in there anyway? I didn't know you were even thinking about it."

"When we talked at lunch, I got to thinking about how a counselor could possibly help with my feelings, so I figured, what the hell, might as well see what they have to say," Gabe answered smiling. "I think tonight I am going to ask my parents if they have ever had any strange or gut feelings and see what they have to say. You've gotten me thinking about all this stuff."

Maggie just smiled, trying to hide her laughter. *I think I'm finally getting through to him,* she thought to herself. *I'm getting to like him. We would make a good team.*

At that minute, the bus pulled up to Gabe's stop. Maggie got up to let him out. "See you in the morning. Have a great night," she said, as Gabe walked up the aisle and off the bus.

* * *

"You too. Let me know in the morning what your parents said," she added.

Nothing interesting went on at Maggie's house that night. She didn't even bother to search the internet about their experiences. She figured there was no reason since they were going to talk to Mrs. Kennedy's friend tomorrow. After dinner, she went back to her room, finished what little homework she had, and turned on the TV, but found nothing worth watching. It was all reruns, so she then got on her iPad and started watching TikTok videos.

* * *

Gabe's house was a little different. When dinner was ready, Gabe's mom called everyone to come down to eat. After dinner started, Gabel began the conversation with a question. "Yesterday morning I had this gut feeling not to take the bus to school. Dad took me instead. Well, you all know what happened to the bus I normally take: a tire blew and the bus went off the road. Thank goodness no one was seriously hurt. Everyone was taken to the hospital with cuts requiring stitches and some broken bones. Even our normal bus driver was back driving this morning with his left arm all bandaged. Anyway, my question is about my gut feeling. I have no idea why I got it or what it really meant. Do any of you know anything about this?"

Gabe's two little sisters both started talking at the same time. "I get weird feelings all the time," said Lucy. Katie jumped in, "Me too, but I have no idea what they're all about."

Gabe's mom turned to him and the girls and said, "I am not sure what they are either. I also get them, but in my case, I usually listen to them. I do know that every time that happens, I find that I am right in listening to them."

"I'm like you too, son," Gabe's dad added. "Sometimes I get gut feelings and I have no idea where they come from. Sometimes I follow these feelings and other times I don't pay any attention to them. It seems you were very smart to listen to yours yesterday morning. Had you not listened, you would have been one of those kids who got hurt."

"So I guess, no-one knows what these odd feelings are all about? Even my friend Maggie had that odd feeling yesterday about not taking the bus, so she didn't. She got her mom to drive her. Last night she had a dream that she was on the bus during the accident and was thrown around and broke one of her legs in so many places and had to be operated on. We think her dream was about what would have happened had she taken the bus."

"Honey, did you have any dreams like that?" asked his mom.

"No, I didn't have any dreams about the accident," Gabe replied.

"Maggie's Gabe's girlfriend. We heard that the two of you talk to each other all the time," his youngest sister said, giggling.

Gabe turned to his sisters, "Maggie is *not* my girlfriend. She's just a friend from school."

His sister kept on, "That's not what we hear at our school. Our friends have told us that you two are together all the time together, that you even know where she lives."

"So, yes I know where she lives but that doesn't mean anything," he replied sounding a little annoyed.

"All right all of you. That's enough. Now finish your dinner and go do your homework. I know none of you have all your homework done," said their mom raising her voice a little.

Well, that wasn't very helpful. Gabe thought to himself as he headed to his room to start his homework.

He wondered if dinner at Maggie's house was just the usual talk about school and what happened during the day. He didn't even know if she talked to her parents about her or his feelings. He imagined what her life at home was like and wondered if she did her normal chores like clearing the table and what she was watching TV. Was she able to put her thoughts about the dream and the strange feeling out of her head and relax for the night? He had trouble focusing much on his homework while daydreams of Maggie and thoughts about their odd feelings kept creeping into his mind.

CHAPTER III

F'or once, Gabe couldn't wait to get to school.

Finally, he saw the bus approaching. *Maybe Maggie got some answers last night,* the thought. If not, at least they would have a chance to talk to the counselor's friend that afternoon. Just then, his stomach started turning, and he got another one of those weird feelings. This one was about his need to tell Maggie that he really liked her and not to put it off any longer. It had been in his mind on the bus yesterday while they rode home together. He almost did it then but somehow stopped himself. *Why don't I think now is the right time? Homecoming is in just a few weeks and I want to take her to the homecoming dance,* he thought. But he felt the twinge again. *This is really starting to get strange. I really need to talk to that lady today. But how do I tell her about this gut feeling with Maggie around?*

Just then the bus pulled up and there she was sitting in the second row with an empty seat beside her. He had no choice but to sit next to her, since she was patting the seat as if to tell him to sit there.

* * *

"So, did your parents talk at all about your gut feeling at dinner last night?" asked Maggie.

"A little but Mom and Dad really didn't know anything. My whole family said they had those kinds of feelings sometimes, but they don't really understand them." Gabe replied. "How about at your house?"

"Same here. Just the normal dinner chat. In fact, there was hardly any talk at all. After dinner I went up to my room and watched a movie to get my mind off the past couple of days," replied Maggie. "I'll just be glad when we can put this whole thing behind us and go back to our normal routines."

"Me too," said Gabe, trying not to look directly at her. On the side, his thoughts were tumbling so quickly that he felt a little overwhelmed. *I just can't tell her how I feel about her right now and there is no way I can tell her about my gut feeling this morning. I can't even tell her I have one because she is going to ask me about it, and I'm not ready to say anything to her.* He steadied himself and continued. "Do you think Mrs. Kennedy's friend will be able to answer our questions about our weird feelings? Are they even the same thing, just using different words?"

Looking directly at him, clearly trying not to smile, she said, "I really don't know. I intentionally didn't look at any of the social media sites last night. I just wanted to try to forget it all for at least one night."

Gabe changed the subject to something more lighthearted, and they passed the rest of the way to school without mentioning the accident again.

Maggie liked Gabe so much but wasn't sure how he would respond to her feelings, so she did her best to hide them. She didn't want to upset him and ruin their friendship. Homecoming just weeks away and she was hoping he would ask her to the dance. She had confided in a couple of their mutual friends but had sworn them to secrecy. Their feedback was that he obviously felt the same way, but she couldn't trust their advice about telling him. He meant too much to her as a friend to risk what they had.

The morning classes went slowly for Maggie, who spent much of the time anticipating their conversation with Mrs. Kennedy's friend after lunch.

It was finally lunch break. She met Gabe at their usual table. She could hear mumbling as she walked over to their table but had no idea what the whispering was all about.

Looking up at Maggie, Gabe said, "Are you ready for this this afternoon's meeting? I'm a little nervous not knowing what it will be all about and if we will even get any answers."

"Yeah, me too. I couldn't even concentrate on any of my classes this morning and my math teacher was going over things that might be on the test next

Monday," she replied, as she took a bite of her cheeseburger.

Maggie tried to focus on eating lunch and had little else to say.

As they were putting their lunch trays back, the bell rang for the end of lunch.

Turning to Maggie, Gabe said, "Well, here we go to find out if we're crazy or not."

* * *

Entering the auditorium, they spotted Mrs. Kennedy way back in the auditorium with some other lady, who looked much older than she did. Upon reaching the two ladies, Mrs. Kennedy said, "This is my aunt, Mrs. Sizemore. Aunt June, this is Maggie and Gabe They're the ones I told you about last night."

Extending her hand, Mrs. Sizemore said, "Nice to meet both of you. I hear you both have questions about strange and gut feelings. Well, I think I might be able to help you both in that area. First I need to hear what happened to you both the other day to question these feelings. Maggie, why don't you start?"

"Thank you for helping us," Maggie said. "To make it short, the other morning I had a strange feeling about not taking the school bus like I normally do, so I asked my mom to take me and she did. When I got to school a friend of mine asked me if I had heard about the bus accident. I hadn't heard anything," Maggie said.

"OK, Gabe, so now tell me what happened to you the other morning," Mrs. Sizemore said, turning to Gabe.

"Well, my story is similar to Maggie's, only I had this gut feeling not to take the same bus. Maggie and I live close to each other, so we take the same bus every day, but this gut feeling told me not to, so I asked my dad and he drove me. I saw Maggie near the school, and she told me her mother drove her. As we were talking, a friend of Maggie's came up and asked us if we were OK. We said 'Yes, why?' She then told us about the bus accident, that it had blown a tire and run off the road, and that some of the kids and the driver were hurt and taken to the hospital. When we heard about the special counselors who would be here to help kids through it all, we decided to talk to one of them. It ended up being Mrs. Kennedy here, which brings us to today and talking to you about our strange feelings," replied Gabe.

Looking at both the kids, Mrs. Sizemore began to talk. "What you both experienced is what is known as intuition. Some people call it intuition, and some call it gut feelings. They are both basically the same thing. Intuitive feelings come from some deep part of us. They are sudden, strong judgments that we can't immediately explain. Like the ones you both had the other day basically telling you not to take the bus. Neither of you had any idea why you had those feelings, but you had them. You both chose to listen to your feelings and get a ride instead. Had you taken it, you both might have been hurt, so, it was good that you listened to them. Many kids and even adults don't listen to their intuitions. Sometimes, not listening to an intuition can lead to problems or trouble."

* * *

"That may be what happened to me the other night," said Maggie. "That night after the accident, I had a dream that I was on the bus when the tire blew. I had cuts all over me and ended up being taken to the hospital in an ambulance. I heard the doctor tell my parents that I had to have surgery immediately because I had many broken bones in my right leg. He told them I needed a metal rod put into my leg. The dream ended there because my alarm went off for me to get up."

Thinking for a minute, before answering. Mrs. Sizemore finally said, "Yes, it is very likely the dream was telling you what would have happened to you had you taken the bus. I haven't heard of very many people having dreams after having an intuition about something, but I'm sure it does happen. Your dream was probably just letting you know how important it is to listen to your intuition. This way you can use your dream as an example about the importance of listening to an intuition. Remember, not all intuitions and gut feelings involve something that could cause harm."

Maggie jumped in, "Oh, you mean like thinking about the need to call a friend, and at that very minute the phone rings. and it is them calling you?"

"Yes. But a gut feeling, or intuition as some people call it, is something we all have more times than not. People tend to ignore them because they don't want to listen to what it's trying to tell them. Many times, it is a warning telling us that something is not right and when listened to, it can save us a great deal of heartache and misery. It feels like a voice inside of us that's telling us to be careful. Both of you are perfect examples of listening to your intuition. Who better than the two of you to tell your friends about the importance of listening to your intuition," concluded Mrs. Sizemore.

With that, Mrs. Kennedy jumped in and said, "I have an idea. Since today is Thursday and the weekend is right around the corner, why don't the two of you get together this weekend and talk about what happened to both of you this week? We'll talk to Mr. Preston and see what he thinks about the two of you talking to the whole school next week about what you both learned about listening to your intuition. I can't think of a better way to let everyone know what intuition is about and the importance of listening to it. Are you guys open to talking about it in front of the whole school?"

Maggie was the first to comment. "I don't know about Gabe, but I was going to talk to my friends anyway this weekend. It would probably save a lot of time and repeating myself if I or we could do it just once. What do you think Gabe? Are you game to give it a try?"

"I, I, guess I could try. As long as we planned out what we were going to say ahead of time and made notes. Why not?" Gabe replied in a nervous voice.

"OK, then. I'll talk to Mr. Preston this afternoon. Maybe my Aunt June would even be able to come and be available to add something to your presentations. Do you think you can come, Aunt June?"

Smiling, Mrs. Sizemore replied, "I can be here whenever Mr. Preston thinks it is best for the entire student body. It is a very important topic that needs to be addressed and not hidden. Who knows how many kids it would help? I bet very few if any young people know about intuition and gut feelings. Count me in."

"OK, you two get back to your classes and we will let you know what Mr. Preston has to say. Please let me have your phone numbers and I'll text you his answer," said Mrs. Kennedy.

Maggie and Gabe gave Mrs. Kennedy their phone numbers and headed back to their respective classes.

* * *

Both Angela Kennedy and her Aunt June headed to the school offices to speak to Mr. Preston about their idea.

"Good Afternoon. I'm Angela Kennedy, one of the special counselors who is talking to the children about the bus accident the other day. My aunt and I would like to speak to Mr. Preston about an idea we have," she said to the secretary.

"Please wait here and let me see if Mr. Preston is available," replied the secretary.

Returning a couple of minutes later, she said, "Yes, he can see you now. Please follow me."

"Good afternoon, ladies, I'm Mr. Preston, the principal. What can I do for you? Did you have problems with any of the students who came to see you about the bus accident?"

"Oh, no, not at all. In fact, the children we spoke to were very understanding and I felt I was able to be of great help to them. The reason we asked to see you has to do with two students who came to us about something related to the accident but that went deeper than that. These two kids were the only ones who did not take the bus that morning. The girl said she had a strange feeling that morning about not taking the bus, and the boyhood a gut feeling that led him to ask his father for a ride. My Aunt June knows a great deal about what these kids were experiencing, so asked her to come in today and talk to them, I'll let her explain."

June said, "Well, to begin with, these strange gut feelings these two kids had were their intuitions talking to them. I explained to them what intuition is and how important it is to listen to those feelings. Not taking the bus was a perfect example of listening to an intuition. They understood what I was telling them, and they said they were going to tell their friends what we discussed. That's when my niece here got the idea about having a school-wide assembly so these two kids could explain it all to the entire school at once. We realize that not all of the kids would understand or even accept it, but we thought it might be worth a try, so, here we are pitching the idea to you."

Looking a little interested, Mr. Preston replied, "Do you think these two kids will actually get up on stage and talk about their experience with their intuitions? I think it is a good idea but am just a little concerned that these two will back out at the last minute. Do you mind telling me their names? I would like to ask them myself."

"Sure. They are Maggie Woodbridge and Gabe Hidalgo," Angela responded.

"Sandy, would you please get Maggie Woodbridge and Gabe Hidalgo and bring them to my office? I would like to speak to them," Mr. Preston said to his secretary.

* * *

"What did you do now that we have been called to the principal's office?" Maggie asked Gabe as they were walking down the hallway.

Looking confused, Gabe replied, "Nothing. I haven't done anything wrong. I wonder if it has anything to do with Mrs. Kennedy and Mrs. Sizemore talking to Mr. Preston about us and their idea?"

"Please come in," Mr. Preston said as Maggie and Gabe entered his office. "I assure you that the two of you are not in any trouble. Mrs. Kennedy and Mrs. Sizemore have told me about their idea of having the two of you talk about your intuitions about the bus accident this week. All I would like to know is if the two of you really agreed to talk to the entire school at a school-wide assembly about your experiences."

Turning to each other, Maggie and Gabe both responded, "Yes," while also nodding their heads.

"We were going to talk to our friends about what we learned and how it is important to listen to what Mrs. Sizemore said were our intuitions. How it is your intuition telling you something important and how you should not ignore them," Maggie said.

Gabe continued, "Yeah. I've had these gut feelings in the past and so have my dad and little sisters. My dad and mom listen to them sometimes and my sisters said they don't always pay any attention to them. They, along with everyone, need to know the importance of listening to your intuition."

"I also need to tell everyone about my dream of what would have happened to me if I had taken the bus. That is why we both realize the importance of all this," concluded Maggie.

Mr. Preston said to all of them, "OK then. "l'll make arrangements and schedule a school-wide assembly sometime next week and let you all know when it is. I suggest Maggie and Gabe get together this weekend and work on what you plan to say."

"Thank you all for bringing this to me. Have a great day. Maggie and Gabe, you may return to your classes now." Mr. Preston said.

As they were leaving, Mr. Preston escorted the two women to the door.

After they were out of the office, Maggie took a few moments to talk with Gabe before going their separate ways to return to their classes. They felt relieved to have a better understanding of their experiences but couldn't help but wonder how it would be to speak to the entire school about it.

"Gabe, are you ready for all this?" She asked.

"Well, I'm not really excited to speak to the entire school, but I think what we have to say is important, so I guess I'll have to manage somehow."

"That's about how I feel," Maggie replied. "I used to get big red splotches on my neck when I had to give a book report in front of the class. I can't imagine speaking in front of everybody." Maggie thought back to her English class just last year when she started to feel like she might pass out just standing in front of the room. She didn't want a repeat of that nightmare. But she felt she had grown enough over the last year to manage to do this.

"You'll be great," Gabe assured her, "You're so natural talking to people. I'm not so sure about how I'll do though." "Well, I guess we'll do it together," Maggie said. "Better get back to call now though. See you on the bus later."

CHAPTER IV

Un the bus after school, Maggie turned to Gabe and said, "I think we really need to talk this weekend and plan what we're going to say at the assembly."

"But we don't even know when it will be," replied Gabe.

"We need to be prepared no matter when it is," she responded. "What if we find out it will be on Tuesday morning or afternoon? We have to be ready ahead of time."

Looking a little more interested, Gabe said, "OK, I guess you're right. So, when do you want to get together?"

"I have chores to do tomorrow morning," Maggie said, "What are your plans for tomorrow afternoon? Sunday morning, we have to go to church, so that is no good either."

"Dad wants me to help with the yard tomorrow. I'll see if I can help him in the morning so I could be free tomorrow afternoon too," Gabe answered.

"OK, why don't we plan for tomorrow afternoon around 2 at my house? Here is my number so you can text or call me when you find out about helping your dad," Maggie responded.

Smiling now, he took out his phone to add her number to his contacts. "Here's my number just in case your plans change. Is there anything you want me to bring?" he asked.

"Yeah," Maggie said, "why don't you do some checking on the internet tonight about intuitions and gut feelings? I'll do the same and then we can compare what we both found and decide what would be best to talk about."

Just then the bus stopped in front of Gabe's house. Before he got up to exit, Maggie added, "Well you know where I live, so I'll see you tomorrow. Have a great night."

"You too" Gabe replied. "Will let you know if I find tomorrow afternoon is good for me," he replied, stepping off the bus. He gave her a wave as he walked up the sidewalk to his house.

Maggie smiled to herself as the bus headed to her home. *Well, I know I like Gabe more than just a friend, but I wonder if he feels the same. I'll have to wait to see what tomorrow brings.*

* * *

After the bus pulled away, Gabe went inside. He could hardly believe how things had changed in the last few days. *This is going to be great,* he thought. *I finally get to spend time with Maggie besides tag school. Guess I'll have to finally tell her that I like her.*

Gabe was daydreaming about spending time with Maggie when he heard his mom call from the kitchen.

"OK everyone, time to come down for dinner," she shouted to Gabe and his sisters.

"OK, Mom. We'll be right down," yelled Gabe.

During dinner, Gabe turned to his dad and said, "Dad, I know you want me to help you with the yard tomorrow. Is there any way we can do it in the morning? I need to help a friend of mine with a project for school in the afternoon."

Looking up from his plate, his dad answered, "Sure, that would be great. The sooner we get it done the better. Besides, if we get it done early enough, I can watch the football game. Notre Dame is playing USC, and I can't wait to see that game. Notre Dame really needs to win this one to have a chance for the title."

Butting in, his mom said, "Since when do you do a school project with someone else? That is the first time I've heard you talk about doing a project with a partner."

"Maggie and I have a special project we are going to do and talk about at a school-wide assembly," he answered.

With a smirk on their faces, his sisters sang, "Gabe's got a girlfriend, Gabe's got a girlfriend. We told you she was your girlfriend."

"Cut it out, twerps," he yelled, turning to his sisters.

"OK kids, cut it out. Now sweetheart, tell me about this special project. You never mentioned it before. What is it all about?" his mom asked.

Gabe felt a little shy about sharing the whole thing with his family, but he took a deep breath and answered his mother's question in detail, explaining everything, including the assembly he and Maggie would spend this weekend preparing for.

Looking completely amazed, his mom replied, "I am totally impressed. I knew about intuitions but never really gave them much thought. You will have to tell your dad and me and the girls everything you learn from your research."

"Yeah, I get gut feelings a lot, but don't know much about them either. I would be interested to hear what you find out," said his dad.

Gabe felt relieved after telling his family about his special project. They seemed genuinely interested in learning more and so was he. It wasn't a topic that came up often, and he couldn't recall a time when such things were even mentioned at home or at school. He became quiet after the discussion, and the rest of the dinner conversation focused on their routine things and on the latest news.

* * *

At dinner that night, Maggie told her parents that Gabe might be coming over open Saturday to help her prepare for a special talk. She explained everything they had learned from the counselor's aunt and Mr. Preston's plans for them to speak at an assembly. Her parents didn't have a lot to say, but her mom seemed interested. All Maggie's little brother, Josh could do was tease her about Gabe being her boyfriend.

After dinner, Maggie returned to her room and began searching the internet about intuition. Whenever she found something that sounded interesting, she printed the pages on the printer.

At about 9:15, her phone pinged. It was Gabe.

"I talked to my dad and we are working in the yard in the morning so I am free to come over tomorrow afternoon," Gabe texted.

Maggie replied, "Great. My parents said it was OK too. See you then. I printed some interesting pages."

Gabe replied, "So have I. See you tomorrow". He ended with a smiley emoji.

That made her smile.

She no sooner finished her text with Gabe when her phone rang. It was Rose.

"Hey, girlfriend. What are you up to tonight?" asked Rose.

"Not much. Just been doing a little research on intuitions and gut feelings for school. Gabe and I have to give a talk at a school-wide assembly in the near future about them because of what we experienced the morning of the bus accident. Gabe's coming over tomorrow afternoon and we're going to make notes so we both don't say the same thing," Maggie answered.

"What? Like I said before, you are one lucky girl. Now tell me all about this talk you and Gabe are going to give," replied Rose.

Again, Maggie explained everything she had told her family about the experience she and Gabe had and the counselors and the school assembly being set up by their principal.

Sounding excited, Rose cut in. "I can't believe that your strange feeling the other morning has turned into a full-blown talk about intuition. You must be very excited about it all. Even getting to spend time with Gabe outside of school."

"Yeah, I am. I guess it's time to tell him how I feel about him. I just hope it doesn't scare him away," she replied, smiling. "Maybe there will be an opportunity to tell him tomorrow. I only hope so. It will be hard to be with him all afternoon and not think about how I feel."

Rose interrupted, "I wish I had that kind of problem. I don't have anyone at school I feel like that about. Then again, I don't know how I would handle it if I were in the same position. I can see your dilemma with the whole thing. And having to work together on the talk and then give the talk, wow, what a challenge." "Yeah, and the hardest part is not knowing how he feels, about me. I think I know, but I'm not sure." Maggie said. "I'll call you tomorrow night and fill you in on what happened and how things went."

"Please do. I can't wait to hear all about it. I'll let you go now so you can finish doing your research," Rose said as she ended the call.

With that call done, she went back to searching, reading, and printing everything she could on intuitions. She even printed some pages that dealt with psychic intuition.

She was getting tired from all the reading she was doing. She turned to the clock in her room and realized why she was so tired. It was 12:17 in the morning. So it was time to shut down her computer and go to bed.

* * *

Gabe spent the night doing research and printing some of what he found to be interesting on the subject. He even printed a page on being psychic.

Knowing he had to help his dad in the morning, he decided not to stay up too late, so he headed to bed around 11 PM.

Sometime during the night, he had a dream about the school bus crash. In the dream, he seemed to be standing on the side of the road when he heard what sounded like a small explosion. Turning his head toward the street, he watched as a school bus blew a tire and ran off the road into a small ditch where it flipped on its side. He rushed across the street to see if anyone was hurt and if he could help. While running, he called 911 to report the accident and give his location. The dispatcher said she would send the police and paramedics immediately.

When he got to the bus, he saw some kids climbing out of the broken windows. He could see that some were bleeding and had torn clothes. He heard one of the kids yelling, "there's a girl inside who looks like she is really hurt. She can't move and is crying."

Gabe realized he could climb up the undercarriage of the bus and help some of the kids out the windows. Just as he got up to the top of the side of the bus, he heard the police and ambulance sirens blaring in the distance, getting closer, but all he could think about was helping the kids out of the bus. Some were covered in blood. Then he saw her. It was Maggie. His heart beat heavily in his chest as he heard her crying and saw how banged up she was with her leg pinned under a seat. He couldn't tell how bad it was. All he could see was that it looked bent in a strange way. He shouted, "Maggie, it's Gabe. I'm coming to get you out."

Through her tears, Maggie yelled back, "No don't. It's too dangerous and I can't move. It feels like my leg is broken and I have cuts all over and I'm bleeding a lot."

At that moment, the police and paramedics arrived. Gabe yelled from the top of the bus, "There's a girl in here who's hurt pretty bad. She says she thinks her leg is broken and I can see cuts where she is bleeding."

"OK, son. Please get down and let us get up there and help her. We have to make sure you aren't hurt," shouted one of the paramedics.

Gabe yelled back, "I wasn't on the bus. The blood on me is from helping some of the kids get out of the broken windows. As for the girl, I don't want to leave her in there by herself."

"I'm right here," said another paramedic, who was standing just behind Gabe. "I see her, and we will get her out, but we *really* need you to get down now and let us handle it."

One of the police officers was on the side of the bus holding his hand up to help Gabe down. "I'm here son. Please take my hand and let me help you down. Let the paramedics get the girl out. You can wait down here."

"OK," replied Gabe as he put his hand out to let the officer help him down.

After the paramedics got Maggie out of the bus, they put a splint one her leg. As they were putting her into the ambulance Gabe asked, "Can I get in there with her? She is my best friend and I know if she sees me there with her, it will calm her down during the ride to the hospital?"

Through her tears, Maggie looked up and saw Gabe standing there. "Please let him ride with me, He's, my boyfriend." She said.

Turning to one of the officers, one paramedic said, "This is very unusual, but if it will help keep her calm, I think we should let him ride with us. If you need to talk to him, I'll make sure he doesn't leave the hospital, but we need to get her there now."

Again, turning to the paramedic, the officer replied, "OK, if you think it would help her then I will follow you. I need to ask him questions about what he heard and saw."

Gabe was already in the ambulance holding Maggie's hand as the paramedic got in and tapped the window for the driver to take off.

"Never knew you considered me your boyfriend," he said quietly. I've always thought of you as my girlfriend but was afraid to tell you because I didn't know what you would think," he added as the ambulance raced to the hospital with the flashing lights and sirens blaring.

Smiling the best she could through her tears, Maggie squeezed his hand and spoke in a soft voice. "I was afraid to tell you too because I didn't know how you felt and if it would scare you away."

During the rest of the trip to the hospital, the two of them just held hands and kept looking at each other. He should tell Maggie was fighting through the pain she felt. He kept a steady, reassuring gaze and smiled too, gripping her hand a little tighter whenever she seemed to wince.

When they arrived at the entrance to the ER, one paramedic turned to Gabe and told him he would have to sit in the waiting room, and that he couldn't go into the area where they were bringing Maggie. The police were right behind them and needed to talk to Gabe about what he heard and saw. The two paramedics then wheeled the gurney into the ER, leaving Gabe standing at the entrance.

"Son, please come inside with me. I need to talk to you about the accident," said the police officer as he escorted Gabe into the waiting room.

"Were you one of the students on the bus? Do you need to see a doctor?" asked the officer as they sat down inside.

"No, sir. I don't need to see a doctor. I wasn't on the bus. I was across the street when I heard this loud boom that sounded like an explosion. I turned and saw that one of the tires on the bus blew out and the bus ran off the road and onto its side. That's when I ran over and climbed up to help the kids get out," said Gabe. "I could tell many of them had cuts and torn clothes. The driver was moving around trying to help some of the kids get out but he looked hurt too. I could see blood pouring down his left arm. One of the kids told me that Maggie was hurt badly and was crying for help, so I was going to try to get to her. That's when you and the other officers and paramedics arrived. That's all I know."

Gabe woke up suddenly shaking from the dream. It was so intense and real. He felt like he had been there. Glancing at his clock he realized it was just almost time to get up and get ready to help his dad. He dressed quickly, grabbed some cereal for breakfast, and headed outside to where his dad was already getting the lawn mower and other yard tools out of the garage. He decided not to tell his dad about the dream. He just wanted to get his work done and hurry over to Maggie's to tell her about the dream and start on their project.

Both he and his dad finished the yard in what was practically record time. The fact that it was a warm, sunny fall day helped.

Gabe went inside to clean up and have a quick bite to eat before heading over to Maggie's house. As he ate, slashes of the dream kept popping into his mind. He replayed the one where she called him her boyfriend more than a few times. The rest of it was harder to think about.

* * *

Maggie finished all her chores quickly that morning. She even had time to help her mother fold some of the week's laundry.

"Honey, what time is your friend Gabe coming over?" her mom asked.

Without looking up, Maggie replied, "We decided around 2 this afternoon. That way I'd be able to finish my chores and Gabe could help his dad with the yard work."

"It's almost 12:30. I think you should go get something to eat and get ready. Where are you going to work on this project? I can make space at the dining room table if that would help." her mom added.

"That might be a good idea, Mom. I was thinking about up in my room, but we may not be able to get comfortable up there. Besides I wasn't t sure how you and Dad would feel about me having a boy in my room all alone."

Chuckling, her mom replied, "I was young once too, my dear. I know what goes on in girls' rooms. Your dad and I trust you and know you wouldn't do anything wrong. Give you another couple of years and that might be another story," her mom added laughing even louder. "OK now, thanks for your help. Go get ready. I'll clean off the table and make sure your dad and brother don't bother the two of you. I can tell this project is very important to the both of you."

"Yes, it is. Gabe and I really want this talk to go well. It is important for everyone to know about intuition," she replied. "I need to go upstairs and get cleaned up a little. Thanks for getting the dining room table set up for us."

After Maggie finished getting ready, she ran back downstairs to grab a quick bite to eat.

"I made a couple of sandwiches for you and Gabe," her mom said turning just in time to see Maggie grabbing something out of the cabinet. "I'll just go and put them on the table for you."

"Great! Thanks, Mom," Maggie said surprised but grateful for her mother's gesture.

No sooner had her mom put the sandwiches on the table than the doorbell rang.

"I'll get it, Mom," Maggie yelled as she ran to the door.

"Am I on time? Couldn't remember exactly what time we agreed to meet," said Gabe.

"Perfect timing," Maggie said. "My mom just put a couple of sandwiches on the dining room table for us. We think that will be the best "Mom said she would make sure we aren't disturbed."

As Gabe followed Maggie into the dining room and sat down in one of the chairs, she asked, "Do you want a drink? We have water, soda, and iced tea."

"Iced tea would be great. Thanks," replied Gabe.

Returning with two glasses of iced tea, Maggie sat next to Gabe. "Why don't we eat first and then start on these pages we both printed."

"Sounds good to me. Besides I'm a little hungry," Gabe said while picking up one of the sandwiches.

As he was finishing his sandwich, Gabe pulled his chair a little closer and started speaking more quietly. Maggie wondered why until she heard what he had to say. He began to describe the dream he'd had last night and went into detail about helping their bleeding classmates get off the wrecked bus and then watching as the EMTs carefully brought her out and took her to the hospital. "I've been thinking about that all morning, wondering if that was letting me know that I was right to listen to my gut the other morning. I know your dream was about you being on the bus so it was interesting that my dream was about you on the bus and me trying to help you. This is all interesting *and* confusing. One thing's for certain, I am so, so glad that neither of us was on the bus." Gabe added that he held her hand on the way to the ER to keep her calm.

Maggie could picture him holding her hand. They had actually imagined that many times. If only she could get up her courage to tell him how she felt about him.

Putting down her glass, Maggie said, "I've been thinking all week about that strange feeling, or should I say intuition, and wondering how many other ones I've had that I never listened to. I remember sometimes when I would be thinking of calling Rose or one of my other girlfriends and at that very moment my phone would ring, and it was them. Was that an intuition? I don't know but I'm hoping we get to talk to Mrs. Sizemore again. I have more questions for her."

"Yeah, me too, but I think we need to get started talking about what we found on the internet before it gets too late," replied Gabe.

Maggie then started, "OK. I'm guessing Mr. Preston will introduce Mrs. Sizemore first. We'll need to ask her beforehand what she plans to say. I hope she doesn't say too much that might take part of our talk away from us. Anyway, if you're ok with it, I think maybe I should start our talk. I'll first describe my strange feeling that morning in the shower and explain that I asked my mom to drive me to school because of it. Then I'll turn to you to tell everyone about your gut feeling that morning and asking your dad to drive you. We can then tell everyone about how Rose came running up to ask us if we had been hurt and told us all about the accident and how it really surprised us."

"That sounds great to me," Gabe replied. "You know I'm a little shy, so you starting, works for me. After you talk about Rose, I can come back in and talk about how surprised and shocked we both were and how the rest of the day all we could think about were the strange feelings we had about not taking the bus and what it all meant," replied Gabe.

She nodded and continued, "I like that and then I'll tell everyone about my dream of having been on the bus and getting my leg all banged up. Then, if you want to, you can talk about your dream. Once we finish that part of our time, I think we should go into what Mrs. Sizemore said about these strange feelings being intuition. All we need to do now is go through all these notes we printed."

Staring down at his notes, Gabe began. "OK, here are some of the notes I found." Maggie watched intently as Gabe started going through each of the pages, he had printed explaining everything he found in detail. She tried to focus on what he was saying instead of just looking into his sparkling brown eyes.

She said, "I've got many of the same notes you have but I found a few more things that go into intuition even deeper. Here's what I found about psychic ability."

She pulled a sheet from her stack of papers printed from the internet. She placed the page in front of him on the table so he could see what she had already read.

"This is good info," Gabe remarked after a minute or so. I'm sure some of the kids in our school may have reached that level of being more *psychic*. We should definitely add some of this. Then once we finish with everything we have to say, we can turn it back over to Mrs. Sizemore and Mr. Preston."

"OK, then all we have to do now is sit down and type out exactly what we plan on saying when it's our turn. I don't think we should have all these pages flipping back and forth. It would be much better if we organized it like we would do with a term paper or essay. We should create an outline," she commented.

Nodding his head, Gabe answered, "OK, I have my laptop with me, or do you think we should just do our own talks and come back together tomorrow to go over what we wrote?"

Looking at the clock, she agreed. "It is getting a little late, so it might be better if we work on our own and you can come back tomorrow to go over what we wrote. I work better when I'm alone anyway. That way I'm not distracted." *I know I wouldn't be able to really concentrate with Gabe sitting here,* she thought.

"OK, what would be a good time for me to come tomorrow? I have nothing to do at home, so any time would be good for me," Gabe said.

She thought for a minute, "On Sundays, we normally go to church and then have our big meal at lunch, so we should be finished by 2 PM. If you could be here by then, I'll make sure I'm finished. If we have to, I'll just tell Mom we need the quiet and will work in my room. That way, mom doesn't have to rush to make sure the dining room and kitchen are all cleaned up for us."

Smiling Gabe replied, "Sounds good to me. I'll have everything done on my laptop and bring it with me. This way if any changes are needed, we can do it right then."

Maggie wished Gabe didn't have to leave, but she had to work by herself in order to concentrate, so she said goodbye to him at the door and watched him walk away toward home before heading back upstairs to work. *If only I had been able to tell him how I feel,* Maggie thought. * * *

On his way home, Gabe kept thinking about Maggie, "Okay guy," *he said to himself,* "you really need to tell her how much you like her. You can't keep putting it off."

The rest of the day and evening Gabe worked on his parts of the presentation. As he was doing some more research, he came across an article comparing intuition with ego. He thought it might be perfect for him to talk about and then

Maggie could go into her part about psychic intuition. With that idea in mind, he created a new page on his laptop and started typing all about intuition versus ego. The more he typed, the more excited he got. The article made intuition so much easier to understand.

It was well after midnight when Gabe finished and printed his presentation. Before he fell asleep, he thought about Maggie and remembered how he felt holding hands with her in the dream. Maybe tomorrow he would find the courage to tell her how much he liked her.

CHAPTER V

Sunday morning was uneventful at Gabe's house. His family sat down for a breakfast of pancakes and sausages prepared by his mother. During breakfast, his mom asked how his presentation was coming and if he felt good about talking in front of the entire school.

"I'm getting a little nervous about standing on the stage and seeing the entire school looking at me, but at the same time, I have learned so much about gut feelings and intuition that I realize how important it is for everyone to hear it," he answered.

"Wow, brother, you sound so excited about intuition. I get them a lot, but don't pay any attention to them. Never thought they meant anything. Maybe you can tell me more about them and why you think they are something I should pay more attention to," said one of his sisters.

Looking at her, he replied, "I promise I'll tell you all about them because they are an important part of our lives. In fact, I learned something very interesting last night about the difference between intuition, gut feelings, and our ego."

Looking a little puzzled, his dad stopped eating and asked, "So what is the difference between a gut feeling and intuition?"

Smiling at his dad, Gabe said, "Nothing. A gut feeling is your intuition talking to you. Your intuition is really your inner voice talking to you. Many people ignore their intuition and end up regretting it. Last week was a perfect example. I told you I had a gut feeling not to take the school bus and asked you to drive me to school. Well, my friend Maggie also had a strange feeling that same morning about not taking the school bus, and as everyone knows, the bus blew a tire and ran off the road. So, our intuition was telling each of us something was going to happen. Had either of us not paid any attention to these feelings, and intuitions, then we would have been on the bus and possibly been hurt or seriously injured. That's why we should never ignore our intuitions, or call gut feelings. Intuition is just our inner voice speaking to us through feelings, sensations, and gut feelings."

Turning toward her son, his mother said, "I'm amazed at what you're saying. I too have had these odd feelings and was not sure what they were. But I'll say, the majority of the time I did listen to what I was feeling and was surprised by what I did or didn't do as a result of these feelings. Thank you for letting all of us know about all this. I for one, will definitely start paying much more attention when I get these feelings."

"Me too, big brother," said his sister, Katie.

"Don't leave me out of all this. I'm definitely going to pay more attention," his dad interjected.

"One last thing you all might want to start doing is making a written note when these feelings come to you. That way you can keep track of what your inner self is saying to you. Mom, if it is OK with you, can you take care of the dishes?

I need to go back to my room and finish up part of the talk before I go to Maggie's this afternoon," Gabe said as he was getting up from the table.

"Sure honey. Go and finish your speech," replied his mom.

Back in his room, he spent the rest of the morning putting the finishing touches on his intuition versus ego talk.

* * *

Over at Maggie's house, it was a typical Sunday morning after church. Her dad was watching the news while her mom was busy in the kitchen.

Maggie was in her room focusing on her part of the presentation. She was working on the difference be intuition and psychic ability.

Her talk started out with what intuition was. She began discussing the strange feeling that led her not to take the bus to school. She didn't know or understand why she was having this feeling, but the sense she shouldn't take the bus key coming up. She went on to write that your intuition is always speaking, through that small inner voice, through hunches and gut feelings that could lead to last-minute changes of plans.

She explained that there truly was no difference between psychic ability and intuition. Psychic ability becomes strengthened the more people pay attention to their intuitions, which allows them to develop and hone it. Many people see psychic ability as something supernatural or some special gift only some people have. I, but in reality, it's just that some people choose to consciously refine and hone the use of their intuition while others don't.

Before Maggie realized it, it was almost 1 pm and she had to get ready because Gabe was coming over again in about an hour. Maggie was stirrup in her room when Gabe arrived. She heard her mother answer the door to let him in and then was surprised when his footsteps sounded on the stairway and a light knock came from her door. She took one last quick glimpse in the mirror, fixed a stray hair that was sticking out, and went to open her bedroom door.

"Hi Maggie," Gabe said. "Your mom said to come on up. She said we'd be working up here today since it would be quieter. Sorry I'm a few minutes let. I lost track of time."

"Oh, OK. She didn't tell me that, but I'm fine. Just don't mind the mess," she replied. Maggie's face suddenly felt warm, and she knew her cheeks were turning red. She hoped he wouldn't notice.

Looking around the room, Gabe said smiling, "If you think this is a mess, you should see my room. Better yet, you wouldn't want to see my room."

"Anyway, let's get down to work. I found something I think would be really great for me to talk about. It was an article on intuition versus ego. I found it extremely interesting. It compared nine items for each. Here, let me show you." Gabe sat down on the window seat, pushing back the cushions as he did, and opened his laptop to let Maggie read about the differences. She took the spot beside him and began reading the article.

After she finished, she looked up and said, "This is perfect. I really like it. Yes, you should definitely use it during your part of the talk. I wrote about the difference between intuition and psychic ability."

Looking a little puzzled, Gabe asked, "Is there a big difference between the two?"

"No," she answered. "People think there is but, it's just that psychic ability is the intuition of a person who has been paying more attention to, using, and developing their intuition. So, like we decided yesterday, we'll start with me talking about my strange feeling about not taking the bus last week and then you talk about your gut feeling about the bus. Then you can ask me to tell everyone about my dream, and once I finish talking about mine, I'll ask you if you had any dreams after the accident. From that, you can tell about your dream and then lead right into the differences between intuition and ego. You can then ask me if there was anything I learned from all this and I can talk about the difference between intuition and psychic ability. When I finish, I'll turn to Mrs. Sizemore and let her and Mr. Preston conclude the presentation. How does that sound to you?"

"Sounds like a plan to me," replied Gabe as he shut down his laptop.

Since it took so little time to decide what to include in their presentation, Maggie wondered what they would discuss next. She fidgeted slightly and felt a little ill at ease. She wanted so much to tell him about her feelings, but simply talked about school and their friends, and a lot of other things that were totally unimportant. After a few minutes, there was a lull in the conversation, and Maggie could feel her nervousness rise as she wondered how to tell her good friend that she thought of him as more than that.

Before the words started to tumble from her mouth, Gabe broke the silence and said to Maggie, "Maggie, I have something to tell you that I should have said a long time ago but wasn't sure how to say it or how you would react. In fact, I even had a gut feeling about it but didn't want to say anything to you."

Looking totally surprised, she asked, "Well, what is it? Now you have me very curious."

"OK. Well, for a long time now, since we first met on the bus last year, I realized that I really like you. Not just because of this presentation but long before all this began. Like I said, I didn't want to say anything because I didn't know how you felt or how you would react. Anyway, I like you more than being just someone to talk to on the bus and at school. There, I finally said it."

Maggie felt a wave of relief wash over her. Smiling and taking Gabe's hand in hers, she said, "Finally. I've been wondering how long it was going to take you to say something. By the way, I've liked you too for almost as long. You have no idea how many times Rose has asked me if I have said anything to you about it. She could see it in both our faces when we are at school around each other."

Just then, a thought came to her that made her giggle. "Gabe, I have a great idea on how to get Rose. You know how she always comes up to me when I get off the bus? Well, Monday why don't we get off the bus together and hold hands? This way we can both see the look on her face when she sees us holding hands. What do you think?"

"I love it, just to see the look on her face! Let's do it," replied Gabe as he looked down at her hand holding his.

They spent the rest of the afternoon talking about their feelings and intuition until it came time for Gabe to head home for supper. Maggie walked him to the front door and said good night and that she would see him on the bus in the morning.

As she closed the door, she leaned back on it and smiled, thinking to herself, *he finally said it. I sensed along that he liked me but could never be sure enough to tell him I felt the same way.*

* * *

Gabe smiled the whole way home. walking back to his house with the same kind of smile. *I feel so much better now that I have finally told Maggie how much I like her. I'm even happier that she likes me too, h*e thought, feeling like he was walking on cloud nine. Before he even realized it, he was two houses from his home.

"So, how did it go? Did the two of you get your presentations done?" asked Gabe's mom as he strolled through the front door.

"Yes, we did. All we have to do now is find out when Mr. Preston is scheduling the assembly. We hope it will be this week. We're both excited. We learned a lot about intuition, gut feelings, psychic ability, and our ego. We both want to let everyone know about all this as soon as possible," he said, sounding excited.

Smiling and nodding, his mom continued, "That's great. I haven't seen you this excited in a long time. Also, did you finally tell Maggie how you felt about her?"

"*Mom*, why would you ask me something like that?"

"I'm your mother and mothers can sense things like that. I've seen the look you give every time you talk about Maggie. Your smile is from ear to ear."

Ginning, he replied, "Yes Mom, I finally told her, and she said it was about time and that she liked me too. Now, it has been a long weekend, and I am really tired, so I'm heading to my room to watch TV. I love you and will see you in the morning. Good night."

"Good night, sweetheart," said his mom as she went back to continue watching her TV show.

Gabe headed upstairs to his room where he turned on his TV and just lay on his bed and relaxed.

CHAPTER VI

Maggie was up before her alarm clock went off. She was too excited to see Rose's reaction when she and Gabe got off the bus holding hands. She showered, dressed, grabbed her backpack, and headed down for breakfast where her mom already had the bacon and eggs cooking.

"Are you all set to give your presentation with Gabe?" her mom asked while flipping the bacon.

"Yes, we are. We just don't know when Mr. Preston will schedule the assembly. We are hoping it will be this week. We should know something today, hopefully," she answered.

"Well, good luck. With all the work you and Gabe put into this, you should do great."

Looking up at her mom, she replied, "Thanks, Mom. Is breakfast almost ready? I'm hungry this morning for some strange reason, and that bacon smells really good."

She hardly got the words out of her mouth before her mom turned with her breakfast plate in her hand. "By the way, you look very pretty today," her mother said. "Is today a special day or something, or is it because you and Gabe finally admitted how you feel about each other?"

"Mom, I just wanted to look extra good today because I think today is the day we are going to find out about the school-wide assembly," she replied. After gobbling down her eggs and bacon. Maggie went back upstairs to brush her teeth and redo her hair one more time. By then, it was time to head outside for the bus.

"Have a great day," her mom yelled as Maggie headed out the door.

* * *

After being awake until late thinking about the weekend and his time with Maggie, Gabe hit the snooze alarm on his alarm clock that morning. His mom had to yell upstairs for him to get up. Realizing he had overslept, he rushed to shower, get dressed, and grab his backpack.

Knowing he was running late, his mom made him a breakfast sandwich he could eat on the way to school. With his breakfast in hand, he rushed out to wait on the bus, which arrived within a couple of minutes.

As soon as he sat down next to Maggie, she asked, "So, are you ready to shock the heck out of Rose this morning,"

"Yeah, I think so. It will be so much fun to see the look on her face when she sees us holding hands."

Both he and Maggie were quiet all the way to school. They could see Rose walking toward the bus as it arrived.

"OK, here goes," said Maggie.

Gabe was the first off the bus. He turned and took Maggie's hand as she stepped off. They began walking casually, hand in hand, toward Rose.

"The look on her face is precious," Maggie said. "She's beaming from ear to ear."

Rose couldn't help but yell as she started running toward her two friends. "What's this? Holding hands? Don't tell me the two of you *finally* told each other how you both felt."

Almost with a laugh, Maggie replied, "Yes, we told each other yesterday after we finished working on our presentations."

Laughing now, Rose said, "Well, it's about time. I think the entire school knew and was waiting to see if the two of you would ever realize it. I can't wait to tell everyone. Oh, yeah. How did the work on the presentations go? Did you guys finish them or were you two messing around all weekend?"

"Yes and no. We finished the presentations and now we just have to wait to see when Mr. Preston has scheduled the assembly. No, we did not mess around all weekend," Gabe answered, looking over at Maggie.

With that, the bell rang for homeroom.

* * *

Mr. Preston's secretary met Maggie and Gabe as they were walking into the school. She said Mr. Preston wanted to see them before homeroom, and not to worry because their teachers have been told they would be late.

She quickly ushered them into the principal's office.

"Good morning, Maggie and Gabe," said Mr. Preston

"Good morning, sir," both replied at the same time.

Mr. Preston continued, "Have a seat, please. I wanted to know how you both still feel about speaking in front of the school at an assembly."

Speaking for the two of them, Maggie responded, "Yes, sir. We worked both Saturday and Sunday and came up with some great ideas to help explain intuition, ego, psychic ability, and gut feelings. I think we have it all covered and in such a way that the rest of the students will understand and enjoy the presentation. All we'd like to know is if Mrs. Kennedy or Mrs. Sizemore would be attending and if either of them planned on speaking. We figured you would open the assembly with a message about the bus accident and how it affected everyone."

"Yes, I do plan on opening the assembly with a few words about the accident and how it really did affect everyone. I've talked to both Mrs. Kennedy and her aunt and they will be attending but don't plan on saying very much. They and I feel the two of you would be the best to handle the presentation because you have experienced these intuitions firsthand. Do you both think you can do it?"

Before Maggie could say anything, Gabe interjected, "Yes sir. We both know we can handle it. We have prepared all weekend and are ready to go. Maggie has certain areas she will talk about, and I have some other areas to talk about. By the time we're done, we really believe all the students will have a much better knowledge of intuition and gut feelings."

"OK, then." Mr. Preston said. I"ll schedule the assembly for tomorrow right after homeroom. I would like the two of you to go straight to the auditorium when the bell rings. I'll let your homeroom teachers know why you aren't in homeroom. This way you two can spend that time with Mrs. Kennedy and Mrs. Sizemore and just relax the best you can. Any other questions?"

Looking over at Gabe, Maggie replied, "No, sir. I think we got it all under control. We're anxious to let everyone know what we have learned and hope they'll both enjoy and learn from what we have to tell them."

"One more thing before you go back to class. Mrs. Kennedy and Mrs. Sizemore are stopping by today around 1 pm. I want the two of you to come to my office and go over some last-minute things with them. I 'll have my secretary notify your teachers that you will be with me and not cutting any of your classes. I really am looking forward to this. I think it's something everyone, students as well as teachers, need to know about," Mr. Preston said.

"Thank you, sir, for the opportunity to let everyone know what we have learned. One last thing. Will the students be asking us questions? We're not ready for that," Gabe added.

Laughing a little, Mr. Preston said, "No, I'll end the assembly after you two finish and let the students know there will be no question-and-answer time. As for anyone asking you questions afterward, I cannot stop that, so you might want to be prepared for that."

"Again, thank you for this opportunity. We'll be able to handle any individual questions after the assembly," replied Gabe, as they were leaving Mr. Preston's office.

"Well, I never even thought about anyone asking us questions after the assembly," Gabe said to Maggie. "I just figured it would be all over and things would get back to normal. Do you think we need to sit down and talk about the kinds of questions they might ask us? Should we go back to Mr. Preston and ask him nicely to tell the teachers not to give us any homework tonight so we can get together after school and talk about what questions we may be asked."

Looking a little concerned herself, Maggie replied, "Yes, why don't we go back right now and ask him?"

They turned around and headed back to the principal's office.

"We need to ask Mr. Preston one more question. Is there a chance we could see him again?' asked Maggie.

"Let me see," responded the secretary.

A minute later, Mr. Preston came out of his office. "I hear you have another question for me. What is it?"

Turning to Gabe, and back to Mr. Preston, Maggie said, "Sir, we would like to know if there was any way you could tell our teachers today not to give us any homework tonight. We would like to get together after school and think of any questions we might be asked and work on possible answers. This way we can concentrate on tomorrow without worrying about doing homework too."

Smiling, Mr. Preston answered, "Sure. Anything to get out of doing homework, eh? Only kidding, of course. I think that makes a lot of sense. This is an important topic and I want your full attention on this. So, yes, I'll make sure your teachers know that whatever homework is assigned tonight, the two of you are excused from doing it. How does that sound?"

Maggie and Gabe looked at each other and just nodded their approval.

"OK, now off to class, the both of you. See you tomorrow morning backstage," said Mr. Preston as he went back into his office.

The rest of the day was somewhat uneventful except that all their friends pointed at them as they walked into the lunchroom hand in hand.

* * *

As the last bell rang to end the day and everyone headed outside to their assigned buses, Gabe caught up with Maggie. "Do you want me to get off at your stop and go to your house to think up any questions that might be asked during the day tomorrow or the rest of the week? All I have to do is text my mom and dad and let them know what my plans are and why. This way we'll be ready with answers."

* * *

"I think that's a good idea," Maggie replied. "This way we can get it all done and relax for the rest of the night instead of being up half the night working on them."

Gabe texted his parents to explain their plans and let them know why he was going to Maggie's house. That way his parents wouldn't be worried.

When they got off the bus at Maggie's stop, she noticed her mom's car in the driveway. *What's mom doing home so early?* she wondered.

"Let me go in first so my mom won't be surprised or upset that you're here with me. It will give me a chance to let her know our plans and what we need to do before the assembly tomorrow morning," Maggie said. She asked Gabe to wait on the porch.

"Hey, Mom, what are you doing at home at this time of day? Is everything OK at work? she yelled as she entered the house.

Shouting back from the kitchen, her mom said, "Yes, everything at work is fine, and I 'm fine. We're slow right now so my boss let me off early."

With a sigh of relief, Maggie said, "Glad everything is OK. I want you to know that Gabe is with me. He's outside. The assembly is tomorrow morning after homeroom, and Mr. Preston said we might get questions during the day and this week, so Gabe is here so we can see if we can think of any questions and have the answers ready. We wanted to do it now so we could both relax tonight. Mr. Preston even talked to our teachers about not making us do any homework tonight so we can finish this and relax."

With a big smile on her face, her mom said, "That's fine, honey. You know your dad and I trust you. We also know this is a very big deal for the two of you and how much you both want to get it right. Let me know if Gabe will be here for dinner so I can set another place for him."

"Thanks, Mom. Let me get Gabe and we'll go to my room. I'll let you know if he'll be here for dinner. It all depends on how much we get done by then," she commented, as she turned and opened the door for Gabe.

Once in her room, they settled down quickly. Maggie began, "I think the first question people will probably ask us is why we gave the presentation in the first place."

"You're right, and I'd say the best answer for both of us is because of what we experienced last week on the morning of the bus crash how we both had those feelings and didn't know why, so we went and talked to Mrs. Kennedy and the next day to Mrs. Sizemore. We can quickly say how much they told us and thought it would be good to tell everyone." Gabe replied.

"Yeah, and we can tell them how Mr. Preston asked if we would be interested in giving a talk to the entire student body. So that was easy. Now what? What if they ask us why we felt it was so important to tell people?" Maggie asked.

"That's easy too," Gabe responded. "We just tell them about our dreams afterward that showed us what would have happened had we been on the bus," Gabe added. "Oh, and another one someone may ask, is where we got all our information."

Nodding she said, "Yeah, it might be a good idea if we wrote down where we found all the information and made copies so we can give them to anyone who wants one. I have a printer downstairs in the study we can use to make copies, say about 12 each, just in case. If we run short, we can always make more."

"Great," replied Gabe.

The two of them spent the rest of the afternoon thinking about all kinds of questions their fellow students might come up with. Before they knew it, it was dinner time. Gabe started packing up his things so he could head home.

Remembering her mother's invitation for him to stay for dinner, Maggie said, "You don't have to go yet. Mom said you could eat here with us if you wanted to. All I need to do is let her know so she can set another place at the table. Do you want to stay?"

Gabe responded with an enthusiastic yes. "I just need to give my mom a quick call and let her know I'm eating here. Then after dinner, I'll head home so we both can relax for the evening." Gabe said. He made a quick call home and then hung up. "She said that was fine but not be home too late since it's a school night."

Maggie yelled downstairs to her mother, "Gabe's staying for dinner. Please set another place."

At dinner, Maggie's parents and little brother bombarded them with all kinds of questions.

"OK, everybody, here's the plan. The assembly and presentation will be tomorrow morning in the auditorium right after homeroom. The entire school will be there, including all the teachers. After that we'll go return to our classes as we always do. We have no idea how long it will last, only that Mr. Preston will start the assembly, and then Mrs. Kennedy and Mrs. Sizemore will speak briefly followed by Gabe and me. When we finish, Mr. Preston will tell everyone who has raised their hands that there will not be any questions answered at this time. He's leaving it up to us to answer any questions any of the other kids have during the day and the week. After that, there are no other plans. We're figuring that everything will go back to normal by Thursday at the latest. I hope that answered all your questions. Gabe needs to head home as soon as dinner is over and I need to go to my room to rest up for tomorrow," Maggie concluded.

Her younger brother kicked her under the table every time Maggie mentioned or looked at Gabe. He also kept giggling without saying anything. Maggie was hoping Gabe didn't think anything about her kid brother's behavior. Otherwise, dinner was uneventful after the initial blast of questions.

As soon as they finished their meal, Gabe grabbed his things, and Maggie saw him to the door. "I hope you have a nice relaxing evening when you get home," she said, as she held the door open.

Turning to Maggie, he said, "I promise I will, and you do the same." With that, he leaned forward and gave her a small kiss on her cheek and said goodnight.

Maggie smiled for the rest of the night. Even when she went to bed, she was still grinning and touching her cheek where Gabe's lips had been for that moment.

* * *

On the way home from Maggie's, Gabe smiled and hummed to himself, remembering their goodnight. As he opened the front door, his mom shouted out from the living room, "I didn't expect you home this early."

"The assembly is tomorrow morning right after homeroom, so we're both going to relax tonight and not do anything. Mr. Preston told all our teachers to give us a break and not assign us any homework tonight so we could relax," he responded as he locked the front door. "So I 'm heading off to my room to do just that. Love you both. Good night."

"Love you too, honey. Get a good night's rest," his mom yelled back.

Gabe spent the rest of the night watching TV and thinking about Maggie.

CHAPTER VII

Tuesday morning was no different from any other weekday morning at Gabe's house, but Gabe was feeling a little jittery as he dressed for school.

* * *

"Are you ready for today?" asked Gabe's mom, as he ate his breakfast.

"As ready as I'll ever be," answered Gabe, between bites of his pancakes.

"Just relax and take a deep breath before you start, and you'll do just fine. I have faith in you," his mom said.

After breakfast, Gabe headed out the door to the bus stop. As the bus arrived, he could see Maggie in her normal seat.

After he plopped down beside her she said, "Are you ready for today? You look more relaxed than I thought you would be."

"Yeah, I'm ready. I'm a little nervous but, I know I'll be fine once we get to the auditorium, and everyone starts coming in. How about you?" Gabe asked.

"I feel great, not nervous at all. Just knowing that what we have to tell everyone is important is enough for me," Maggie replied as she reached for his hand. "We'll both do great."

Once at school, Rose came running up to them as usual, wanting to know if they were scared or nervous at all. Both Maggie and Gabe shook their heads.

After a quick conversation, the bell rang for homeroom. Rose turned to Maggie and said, "Come on. I'll walk in with you."

"No, Gabe and I won't be going to homeroom this morning. We have to report to the auditorium," answered Maggie.

Rose turned and headed to her homeroom, and Maggie and Gabe walked toward the auditorium to meet Mr. Preston, Mrs. Kennedy, and Mrs. Sizemore.

Backstage they saw both Mrs. Kennedy and her aunt but not Mr. Preston.

Just then they heard Mr. Preston on the school's PA system. "Good morning, everyone. This morning will be a little different from usual. After homeroom, everyone will please head to the auditorium for a special presentation. All the teachers have been briefed and will accompany each class beginning with the ninth graders and then the tenth, eleventh, and finally twelfth. All those scheduled for the gym right after homeroom will also head to the auditorium. There will be no gym classes during first period today."

Mrs. Sizemore turned to both Maggie and Gabe, "Are you two ready for your big moment? Mrs. Kennedy will talk right after Mr. Preston, then I'll say a few things about how we met and then turn it over to the two of you. Who's going to go first?"

Gabe pointed to Maggie as she said, "I am. We have it all worked out. We'll be going back and forth starting with my strange feeling and then Gabe's gut feeling last week. We'll then talk about the dreams each of us had later that week and finally discuss intuition versus ego and intuition versus psychic abilities."

Looking totally surprised and shocked, Mrs. Kennedy said, "Wow, I'm impressed. It sounds like the two of you did a great deal of research on this subject. What do you think, Aunt June?" She asked, turning toward Mrs. Sizemore.

"I'm also impressed. Now I am really looking forward to hearing what you both have to say," Mrs. Sizemore replied. "Here comes Mr. Preston now. It's almost time.

Walking up to the four of them, Mr. Preston said good morning and asked how everyone felt and if they were nervous at all.

Gabe raised his hand and said, "I am a little, but I think by the time it's my turn to speak, I'll be fine."

Looking down at his watch, Mr. Preston said, "Well it's about time for the bell to ring, so take a couple of deep breaths and relax. I know you will both do wonderfully."

Just then, the bell sounded, and they heard the noise of kids in the hallways heading toward the auditorium.

Mr. Preston headed onto the stage, waited until everyone was seated, and then asked them all to please quiet down.

Once the room went silent, Mr. Preston stepped up to the microphone and welcomed everyone.

"Good morning again. I'm sure some of you may know the reason for this special assembly but some of you may not. Last week, one of our buses blew a tire and ran off the road on the way here. Thank goodness no one was badly injured, just a few bumps, bruises, and stitches. I'm glad to see that those of you with broken bones are here this morning and are healing. Even your driver was treated, stitched up, and released from the hospital. He handled that bus like a pro and prevented possible major injuries. He was even back on the job the next morning driving some of you to school. As a result of that accident, I instructed my staff to bring in some counselors to talk to any of you who were upset about what happened or distressed about what would have happened had it been your bus. I spoke with many of the counselors after the two days they were here, and they were impressed by the resilience of the many students who came to talk to them. With their help, you left feeling more relaxed and more comfortable. I just want to thank all of you. I am proud of how well all of you and this school handled the accident. I've asked one of the counselors to come this morning and share a little about what she experienced talking to some of you. Mrs. Kennedy, would you please step up and tell everyone what you experienced as one of the counselors."

"Thank you, Mr. Preston. Let me begin by saying how much I appreciated being asked to come and speak to many of you students who felt the need to talk after the accident last week. I've spoken to some of the other counselors who were here. They related that most of your questions had to do with concerns about how to handle the feelings you were having. Many of you were even concerned about the buses in general. Could this happen to any of the other buses? Were the buses always being inspected for problems like the tires or other mechanical problems? Many were also upset because their friends had been on the bus and for a while, they had no idea how bad the accident was or if anyone had lost their life. Even after some of you heard that there were no serious injuries or loss of life, you still couldn't get the picture out of your head. We counselors sat and talked to everyone for as long as was needed. Most of us recognized that we had a positive effect on those we saw. There was one young lady who came to me with a completely different question that, in all honesty, I could not answer. Just as I was getting ready to tell her I knew someone who might have an answer to her question, a friend of hers came in, and she called him over to where we were sitting. He too had almost the same question. I asked both of them if they could come back the next day, and I would bring my gun with me to help answer their questions. They agreed to come back the next day. The next day I brought my aunt, Mrs. Sizemore, who is with me here today. Aunt June, please come out and join me."

Mrs. Sizemore walked onto the stage. "Good morning, everyone," she said. "I'm very pleased to be here. I was able to help these two children with their questions. As a result, both my niece and I felt it would be a great idea to have these two students talk to all of you about their experiences. Mr. Preston agreed and so did the two students. Neither Mrs. Kennedy nor I want to take anything away from their presentation. I'm sure many of you know one or both of them. Please welcome Maggie and Gabe."

Gabe was surprised that Mrs. Kennedy failed to mention what their questions were about, and that Mrs. Sizemore said so little about their discussion. He could feel his legs wobbling slightly just before they came out onto the stage. He wondered if Maggie felt nervous. He squeezed her hand for a second to steady himself and ease any nerves she might have.

As the two of them walked onto the stage, everyone in the assembly clapped and yelled their names. Mr. Preston had to come back on stage and to ask everyone to please quiet down. Students,

Maggie and Gabe, have something important to discuss. Let's all be quiet and listen." he said.

* * *

Maggie was glad Gabe had clasped her hand. She felt as if her nervous energy was calmed. She stepped up to the mic, took a deep breath, and began. "For those of you who don't know, me, my name is Maggie Woodbridge, and I'm a junior. I want to tell you about something really strange that happened to me last week. I was taking a shower, getting ready for school, when a weird feeling came over along with the thought that I needed not to take the school bus that morning. What made it even stranger was that I really enjoyed riding the bus and talking to my friends on the way here. Anyway, my feelings was so strong that I asked my mom if she would please take me to school. She drove me that morning and it wasn't until I got here that I was told about the accident. It turns out I wasn't the only one who didn't take the bus that morning."

Maggie glanced over and nodded to Gabe, who quickly took her place at the podium. "Hi, my name is Gabe Hidalgo," he said. "I'm a junior here too. That same morning, after I finished getting ready for school, I was in our kitchen eating breakfast when I got this really strong gut feeling about the school bus. My gut said not to take the bus. I asked my dad if he would drive me since he goes right past the school on the way to his work. He did. When my dad dropped me off, I saw Maggie and told her about not taking the bus. That's when she told me she didn't take it either. While we were talking, Maggie's friend Rose came running up to us and asked us if we were OK. We had no idea what she was talking about. That's when she told us about the bus accident. Maggie and I looked at each other and couldn't believe that both of us had feelings not to take the bus in the morning and the bus had an accident. If that wasn't enough, I'll let Maggie tell you about a dream she had after that day."

Returning to the microphone, Maggie continued the story. "I had a dream the night after the accident that I had been on the bus that morning. It was so vivid, I felt like the dream was real. In the dream, I got all cut up and my leg was broken badly. I was put on a stretcher and taken by ambulance to the emergency room of the hospital. Once in the ER, I could hear the doctor telling my parents that my leg was broken in several places and that I needed emergency surgery right away to have a metal rod put in. The last thing I remember in the dream was being wheeled into surgery. That's when I woke up. So, not only did I have a strong feeling not to take the bus but also had a dream about what probably would have happened if I had taken the bus." A shiver ran down Maggie's spine as she remembered how intense the dream had felt. She was glad it was Gabe's turn to speak again.

"Maggie wasn't the only one with a dream after the accident," said Gabe, returning to the mic. "I had a dream a couple of nights later. In my dream, I wasn't on the bus but was standing across the street. I heard the tire blow and when I turned, I saw the bus run off the road and fall on its side. I ran across the street, climbed up the side of the bus and helped some of the kids get out through the windows. There was a lot of commotion and kids bleeding. We were doing our best to pry open the windows to get people out. That's when I saw Maggie. She was bleeding and pieces of glass were all over her. It looked like one of her legs was pinned under a seat. I was trying my best to climb into the bus through one of the windows when I was pulled back by an officer, who said I had to get out and let them handle the situation and get the young lady out. All I saw after that was Maggie being put on a stretcher with what looked like a piece of wood strapped to her one leg. I was able to ride in the ambulance with her to help keep her calm. The ambulance rushed us to the hospital where Maggie was taken to be examined."

Hearing Gabe's description again, Maggie was even more thankful she wasn't on the bus that day.

Gabe motioned for Maggie to return to the podium. She continued, "When Mr. Preston said he was making arrangements for counselors to come and talk to anyone who felt a need to discuss the accident, I thought that would be the best time to ask about my strange feeling, so I went Mrs. Kennedy with my question and Gabe joined us later. She really didn't know how to explain her feelings, so she asked us to come back to see her aunt, Mrs. Sizemore, the next day. Mrs. Sizemore explained that what we were experiencing was our intuition. Both Mrs. Kennedy and Mrs. Sizemore spoke with Mr. Preston, and he talked to us about us giving this talk to the entire school, so here we are." Maggie looked down briefly at her notes and then continued. "We're here to talk about intuition, which is described as the initial gut feeling or first impression you may have about a person, place, or event. The feelings Gabe and I experienced about not taking the bus are a perfect example of intuition at work. Sometimes intuition comes as a broader feeling that something isn't quite right about a person or situation. Basically, it's that you know something just isn't right, but you can't explain why. Gut feelings are something we all have, but more often than not we ignore them. Often our intuition is telling us something isn't right, and we may not want to hear that. It feels like a voice inside of us that's telling us to be careful. I'm going to go into a little more detail about intuition in a couple of minutes, but I would like Gabe to talk a little about intuition versus ego first."

Gabe stepped forward again and said. "Hopefully we all know what our ego is and basically know what a gut feeling is. "But I want to explain the difference between the two just to be sure everyone gets it. Your intuition speaks to you in a way that's calm, quiet, and detached, while your ego comes across as loud, forceful, and attached to strong emotions. Your ego comes as a stream of thoughts while your intuition usually gives you a single statement or idea message. Last week, when Maggie had her weird feeling and I got my gut feeling, there were no loud or forceful words, just a calm single knowing about not taking the bus that morning. Our ego didn't even get involved. The feelings we had didn't go on and on, There was just one simple idea." Don't take the bus". With your intuition or an intuitive idea, it just feels right. Even though you don't understand why, you just know it's right. Your ego, on the other hand, would come across as saying something logical, but not necessarily true. Maggie and I could have listened to the ego and said, 'Not riding the bus makes no sense. I'm going to go the usual way to school.' But we're really glad we decided to pay attention to our intuition instead. From what I've read, your ego wants to keep you the same, while your intuition wants you to grow and expand. Your ego may even try to imitate intuition, so you have to know the difference and pay attention to your feelings. If you ever get a gut feeling like I did or an eerie feeling like Maggie's, it's your intuition talking to you, so I would suggest that you listen to it. I have to admit, I've had many gut feelings and never listened to most of them, but after last week and the bus accident and everything I've learned as a result, I'll definitely listen to my intuition from now on." Gabe gazed over at Maggie and added.

"Now Maggie will talk a little about psychic ability and intuition."

"Thanks, Gabe," she said, taking the spot in front of the mic again. "I'm sure many of you have heard about or known a person who had psychic abilities. Some of you may have envied those people and others may have just brushed them off as fakes. Well, believe it or not, everyone has psychic abilities. I know many of you are thinking. 'She's nuts. I don't have psychic abilities. I'm not psychic. I even question if I am intuitive.' Well, guess what, everyone is intuitive. We all have gut feelings, which means we are all intuitive. Since we all have had intuitive thoughts about an event or person, then we all have psychic abilities. Psychic ability is nothing more than paying attention to, developing, and honing your intuition. Psychic ability appears to be supernatural, but it isn't. It's just that some people choose to use their intuition consciously and actively. It's like everything else, the more you work at it, the better you become. Now, some people are naturally gifted with this ability, just like those who might be natural athletes, singers, or even musicians. Then there are those who may develop their psychic ability after a major life change or traumatic experience. There are also those who suddenly find they are psychic. That's because they're finally noticing their intuition. Their sixth sense has been there all along. Hopefully, Gabe and I have been helpful in describing what gut feelings are encouraging you and not to brush them off. Intuition is a part of us that we cannot ignore. We only dreamt of what would have happened to us had we been on the bus last week. Speaking for both of us, we are very glad we listened to our strange feelings, our intuitions. We have both learned not to ignore our intuitions in the future and neither should any of you. Speaking for both Gabe and me, I just hope you all learned something today and take what we said to heart. Thank you."

Everyone started clapping and some even raised their hands like they were wanting to ask questions.

Mr. Preston took the mic for a final announcement. "I see many of you raising your hands. Mrs. Kennedy and Mrs. Sizemore will be available the rest of the day in the library for anyone who wants to see them. I ask the teachers to please let your students go and talk to Mrs. Kennedy and Sizemore if they feel the need. As for Maggie and Gabe, they'll be returning to their normal classes just like all of you will. I know you probably have questions for them too, but I ask that you please give them a little room and sometime before you start inundating them with your questions. If I see it's necessary to provide an opportunity for them to answer your questions, I'll set some time aside tomorrow. Thank you. Now please return to the next scheduled classes."

Backstage, Maggie and Gabe were talking with Mrs. Kennedy and Mrs. Sizemore when Mr. Preston walked up to them.

He said, "I just want to tell the two of you that you both did an excellent job with your presentations. I am very proud of both of you as I believe Mrs. Kennedy and Mrs. Sizemore are."

"That's what we were both telling them," said Mrs. Sizemore. "My niece here doesn't know that much about intuition and psychic abilities, but as one who does, I was extremely impressed with these two young people. It was obvious they did a great deal of research on these subjects."

Nodding in agreement, Mr. Preston added, "I was also so impressed with how you both handled yourselves today. Although you are juniors, when the time comes and you start applying to colleges, please let me know, I want to write letters of endorsement for each of you. Also, please let me know if you get too many questions during the day today. Like I said on stage, I'll schedule times tomorrow for you two to answer questions. If need be. Now off to class for both of you. Mrs. Kennedy and Mrs. Sizemore, I would like you both to stop by my office so we can talk a little more."

"Give us a few minutes and we will meet you in your office. I want to talk to my aunt first if that's OK with you," replied Mrs. Kennedy.

"Sure, see you in a few minutes," said Mr. Preston.

Maggie and Gabe hurried away to head back to class. She held his hand until they parted ways to go to different parts of the building.

* * *

When Maggie and Gabe found each other in the cafeteria at lunch, they had a similar story to share. Separately they were bombarded with questions ranging from, what did the gut feeling feel like to how was it working with each other to how scared were you when you had the dreams. If that weren't enough, they were also teased and put down.

"I couldn't believe people," Gabe said. I got so many crazy comments and questions that I think we need to talk to Mr. Preston about how to handle everything and still be able to concentrate on classes."

"Let's go talk to talk with Mr. Preston right after lunch," Maggie suggested.

Three boys approached their table laughing and smirking. One of the boys, Larry, asked, "Hey, Maggie, do you have a crystal ball in your backpack? I want to know if we're going to beat Oceanside High in football this Friday night."

Another boy laughed and chimed in, "Hey Gabe, are you some kind of voodoo doctor? If so, I'll trade you my pizza for a voodoo doll of my biology teacher. I'd like to stick a couple of dozen pins in her ass."

Maggie looked at Gabe and said, "Just ignore them. They're a bunch of morons."

The third boy decided to join in the fun and said, "Yo, psychic, how many fingers do I have behind my back?" Bringing his hand from behind his back with the middle finger extended, he shouted. "One," as all three roared with laughter.

Maggie and Gabe got up, dropped off their trays and walked out.

Turning to Maggie, Gabe said, "Whatever! Some people just don't get it. Let's just head to talk to Mr. Preston like we planned."

As they entered the secretary's office, Mr. Preston happened to see them. He came out of his office and said. "How rough has it been for you two this morning?"

"Very," said Maggie. "Neither one of us could concentrate on our work. Kids were even whispering to us in class asking questions. I even got a couple of notes, including some nasty ones. I just threw them away. Some called me a suck-up, others said 'slut', and in one of my classes the words 'kiss-ass' were on the board."

Gabe clenched his fists when he heard what people had written to Maggie. He felt like putting a fist into a wall or maybe into the face of the guys who wrote those kinds of things to the girl he cared about so much. He knew she wouldn't want him to get upset, so he did his best to calm now.

Mr. Preston looked a little shocked by what she said too. He said. "OK, we have a small conference room on the other side of the secretary's office. Why don't both of you go get your backpacks and books out of your lockers, and I'll have my secretary show you to the conference room where you can relax for the rest of the day. I'll even make arrangements to have one of my staff drive you both home, if you want instead of taking the bus, I 'm very sorry, I didn't expect this kind of reaction. Let me see what I can do. Please follow me."

Gabe and Maggie walked behind him into the outer office where the school intercom was located. Mr. Preston motioned for them to take a seat while he went to the PA system.

"Good afternoon, students." He said. "This is Principal Preston. I'm not at all happy with the way some of the students have been treating Maggie and Gabe since the assembly this morning. Their presentations were my idea, not theirs. They both agreed when I brought up the subject last week. My goal was to hopefully show each of you the importance of listening to your intuition. If you want to blame anyone, then come to me and not to the students who just tried to help all of you. If this continues tomorrow, those involved will be suspended. Legitimate questions are fine, but I will not tolerate anything else, especially the nasty notes and writings I've been told about. I hope I've made myself perfectly clear."

Gabe wasn't sure if the announcement would help or hurt them. He and Maggie followed the secretary to the conference room and spent the rest of the day quietly. They both decided to accept the ride home from one of the staff members after school.

As Maggie got out of the car at her house, Gabe shouted, "I'll call you tonight if you're OK with that."

"Yeah, that would be great," she replied as she walked toward her front door.

After Gabe was dropped off, he went to find that no one was home yet, so he went to his room to relax. He was still pretty agitated about what the other students had written about Maggie and found himself unable to sit still without something to occupy his. He decided to call Maggie.

When Maggie's phone rang, she answered, she smiled and said, "I didn't expect a call from you. I figured you went home and crashed."

"I did," he replied, "but the more I thought about today, the more I couldn't lay back and relax. I'm both happy and mad if that makes any sense."

Maggie said, "I know just how you feel. I really thought our presentations went great. I was so proud of both of us. Even at the end when almost everyone started clapping and raising their hands like they wanted to ask questions. I never expected what happened after that and the rest of the day." I don't even feel like going to school tomorrow if it is going to be anything like today."

"Yeah, I totally agree," Gabe replied. "I felt so good after it was all over. I even felt like I got my confidence back. Then it seems it all went to hell the rest of the day. I even got quite a few text messages calling me all kinds of names. I think there were only two or three that actually said something positive. I know my parents are going to ask me tonight at dinner how it all went. I'm not too sure I want to talk about the negativity." He bit his lower lip as he tried to imagine what on earth he was going to say to them.

Since they were on a video call, he could see Maggie nod in agreement. "I was thinking almost the same thing," she said. "I think I'm just going to tell them how great it went and how proud Mr. Preston was and how he said he was so pleased he was going to write each of us a recommendation to whatever college we applied to next year. Then I plan on leaving it at that. Maybe I'll say that some of the kids asked us questions during the day but nothing about all the negative notes and messages. I think that would be the best thing for both of us. Keep it all upbeat and positive. I see no need to get our parents all upset and have them blame Mr. Preston."

"I think we both need to go to see Mr. Preston before school tomorrow and let him know about all the negative messages too," he replied.

"Agreed," said Maggie, nodding. "I hear my mom calling me for dinner. I'll see you on the bus in the morning."

"OK, have a great night, and try to relax," he said as he ended the call and turned off his phone.

Gabe followed their plan and told his parents exactly what he and Maggie had discussed about how well things went. He remained quiet about the rest even though it was difficult to hold all his feelings inside after getting so upset.

After dinner, he went upstairs and watched TV but couldn't really focus on even his favorite programs. He had a restless night's sleep and hoped Maggie was doing better than he was.

* * *

CHAPTER VIII

Early the next morning, still half asleep, Gabe reached over to turn off his alarm clock. He let out a deep sigh and went off. Gabe felt more than a little hesitant about going to school, but he knew he had to face everyone.

These feelings lingered as he dressed for school and had breakfast. He remembered what he and Maggie talked about yesterday afternoon on the way home and knew he had to go and confront whatever was going to happen.

As he got on the bus, Maggie was in her usual spot, waving to him. "So, how are you this morning?"

Sitting down and turning toward her, he replied, "I was very hesitant about even going this morning, but I remembered our talk yesterday and figured I might as well face things and see what happens."

"Me too. I didn't want to get up and face everything this morning," Maggie said.

140

As the bus arrived at their school and they got off, a couple of kids came up to them and asked if they would answer questions about yesterday's assembly.

Looking a little relieved, Maggie said, "Sure. We were worried you might start teasing or making nasty remarks to us."

Larry, one of the boys who teased them the day before in the cafeteria, said, "Oh no. First off, I want to apologize for how we acted yesterday in the cafeteria. We heard what Mr. Preston had to say in his announcement, and even all the teachers talked about how well you both did and said everyone should be glad and listen to what you had to say. Our teachers agreed about how important it is that we listen to our intuitions more and not ignore them. I really don't think you'll hear much today that would upset either of you. Talking with other kids after school, many of us realized that what you did and said was necessary. In fact, in most of the classes yesterday, we talked about intuition and gut feelings. We're glad you spoke up. It really did help us, so, can we ask you a couple of questions before the bell rings?"

Gabe was shocked by what Larry was saying. "Wow, we hadn't heard any of that, only the negative comments and texts. Sure. You can ask us anything you want."

Continuing, Larry asked Gabe, "You talked about a gut feeling. What was it like? Was it a pain in your stomach or a thought or what?"

"It was very similar to what Maggie had," Gabe said. "A strange feeling. It was like something just popped into my head that said. 'Don't take the bus.' Nothing else. That was it and I felt it only once. I've had gut feelings in the past and didn't think much of them, but, this time, something told me to listen to this feeling. I did and, trust me, I'll listen every time from now on," Gabe added.

Maggie interjected, "Mine was pretty similar. Only it was more of an overall strange feeling. As we learned over the weekend with our research, they are really the same thing. As for me, I haven't had feelings like this before, so it kind of scared me. That's why I went to my mom and asked for a ride to school. With everything we learned this past

142

weekend, I too will begin listening to my intuition more in the future."

Larry's friend Mike said, "Thanks guys. I think that helped us to understand a little better. We're glad you felt strong enough to talk to everyone about it. We also heard that Mr. Preston had asked you to do the presentation and that it was his idea, not yours. Many of the other kids thought it was your idea so you could gain points with Mr. Preston.

Gabe felt himself start to relax during the conversation, He said, "Thank you, guys, for letting us know what Mr. Preston announced and what the teachers discussed. We spent most of the day in the teachers' conference room, so we didn't have to listen to all the negative comments and posts." He didn't let the boys know that he and Maggie listened to the announcement before they went into the conference room.

Larry and his friends left Gabe and Maggie and headed into the school. "Guess today may not be as bad as we thought," Maggie said to him. "I 'm feeling a little better. How about you?"

"Yeah, me too," Gabe responded with a little smile. "I was all ready to go to see Mr. Preston and ask if we could spend the day in the conference room again."

Just as he finished, the bell rang for homeroom. "See you at lunch," said Maggie as she turned and hurried into the school.

As Maggie and Gabe entered the front door of the school, they were met by Mr. Preston's secretary. "Mr. Preston would like to see both of you in his office now before you go to your homerooms."

Looking at Maggie, Gabe shrugged and said, "Great. What did we do now? School hasn't even started yet."

Mr. Preston's secretary replied, "Nothing. Mr. Preston just wants to see how the two of you are doing and if you feel you should go to your classes today or stay in the conference room again."

After the secretary ushered the two of them into the principal's office, Mr. Preston said, "Good morning, Maggie, and good morning to you too, Gabe. How are you both feeling this morning? Are you ready to go to your classes or would you rather stay in the conference room again today until things settle down a little?"

Gazing over at Gabe, Maggie said, "We were just talking to a few of the kids outside, and it seems everyone got the wrong impression about the assembly yesterday. The word must have gotten around that you asked us to give the presentation instead of us asking you if we could do it. That's why kids were saying what they said and wrote yesterday. Seems that a great many thought we were trying to get brownie points and get in good with you and our teachers. When people heard it was the other way around, attitudes toward us changed. We were told this morning that there were many kids who had some real, in-depth questions about gut feelings and psychic abilities. One of the kids outside even said that he really believes in this stuff and has been getting more and more information and wants me to talk to him when we both have the time about what he thinks maybe he having psychic abilities. So, speaking for myself, I want to go to my classes today and see what other kinds of questions there might be."

"Me too," Gabe added. "Since everything has changed today, I think it's important for Maggie and me to be there for anyone who wants to talk to us. Just like you had the counselors here last week."

"OK then'" the principal said. "Why don't the two of you just go over to the conference room and sit out homeroom so you can relax a little? I'll send one of my staff to let your homeroom teachers know that you are here and will be going to the rest of classes today." Mr. Preston called his secretary and asked her to take Maggie and Gabe to the conference room. He motioned for one of his younger staff members and added, "Please let their homeroom teachers know that Maggie and Gabe are here in school today and are with me until the end of homeroom at which time they'll go on to the rest of their classes today."

* * *

Sitting in the conference room, Gabe and Maggie started talking about what to expect and how they would handle any questions, other students had for them.

"Larry and Mike and their friends really changed my way of thinking about today," said Maggie.

"I know. I was really nervous about coming in this morning. I didn't want to hear or read any more crap from everyone. I had enough of that yesterday. I was so tempted to just stay home," replied Gabe. "I do have one more idea. If we get too many questions, I think we should see Mr. Preston again and ask him if he could set us up in a room and let anyone with a question or questions come to us. Maybe use the cafeteria. What do you think about that idea?"

Nodding in agreement, Maggie grinned and said, "Did I hear you right? You actually had a good idea and didn't leave it up to me. Yeah, I think that would be perfect. Mr. Preston could let the teachers know. Maybe we ask him to make an announcement before we go to our next class that we would be available to answer any and all questions tomorrow in the cafeteria during homeroom, and anyone who wants to talk to us could get the OK from their homeroom teacher and come to the cafeteria. This way, we can concentrate on our classes today and get back into the groove."

"That's even a better idea. I think we should go ask him now before homeroom ends so he can make the announcement," Gabe said, as he stood up.

Seeing Mr. Preston in his office, Gabe and Maggie asked his secretary if they could talk to him about their idea.

Mr. Preston notices them and waives them into his office. "Is there something else you two need?"

Looking at Gabe, Maggie said, "This is your idea, so you go ahead and ask Mr. Preston."

"Sir, Maggie and I were talking just now in the conference room and came up with an idea about all the questions we will probably get today you know about gut feelings, intuition, ego, and psychic abilities. Anyway, what if you made an announcement before the end of homeroom asking everyone to hold their questions until tomorrow so we can get back into our classes? Then tell everyone that tomorrow, during homeroom, we'll be available in the cafeteria for anyone who has real questions for us. Anyone wishing to talk to us can come to the cafeteria during homeroom and ask us their questions then. Andy could ask the teachers to let them go. This way no one is missing any classes, and we can get back to our regular classes and not be bombarded all day."

Nodding Mr. Preston replied, "I think that would be a great idea but tomorrow is a teacher workday, so there is no school. Why not schedule it for the day after tomorrow? There are still about 20 minutes left in homeroom so it would be easy for me to make the announcement. I cannot promise you won't get any questions today, but this might help. OK, go ahead and go back to the conference room. I'll make sure the speaker in the conference room is on so you can hear my announcement. Then when the bell rings you both can head to your first class."

As they turned to leave Mr. Preston's office, Maggie turned and said, "Thank you, sir. We really appreciate everything you're doing to help us."

As soon as they left the office, Gabe took Maggie's hand in his, and they headed back to the conference room. Before they arrived, they heard the announcement coming over the PA system.

The principal cleared the air to make certain *everyone* knew the assembly was his idea and added the information about holding their questions until the day after tomorrow since there was no school tomorrow due to a teacher's work day.

* * *

As Maggie walked into her first class, she noticed a comment on the whiteboard, that read," We are sorry we were nasty to you and Gabe yesterday." She had just read those words when she turned to take her seat and the entire classroom started clapping and yelling, "Way to go Maggie. You did great!"

During class, five notes were passed to her with questions about psychic abilities. Maggie pointed to the clock, indicating she would answer them after the class ended. Maggie smiled to herself. She felt both relieved and happy about how much things had changed since yesterday.

As Gabe was walking to his class, his phone sounded, indicating he had a text message. Stopping in the hallway, he took out his phone. He saw six messages. All basically said they were sorry about harassing him, and most added that they wanted to ask him questions at lunch. He quickly responded to each one with a thumbs-up emoji.

Gabe was waiting for Maggie at the entrance to the cafeteria. "So how was your morning?" he asked as she approached him.

"It was pretty good, actually. There was an apology on the board as I went into my first class and some of the kids had questions in between classes. How was your morning?" Maggie asked.

"Mine was good too. I had a few text messages telling me they were sorry for treating us badly yesterday and wanted to know if they could ask me questions during lunch," said Gabe.

Both of them went through the line and got their food. As they sat down at an empty table, a few other kids asked if they could sit with them and ask a couple of questions about their presentation.

Pete was the first one to speak up. "You talked about gut feelings yesterday. Was that the first time you ever had a gut feeling? What did it feel like? Was it like someone was yelling at you?"

Smiling at Pete, Gabe answered, "No, I've had these kinds of feelings before but never really gave them much thought. The one last week was no yelling, but simply a thought that I should not take the bus that day. I didn't hear any voices, I just had that one thought. I have no idea why I actually paid attention this time and asked my dad to drive me. I just told him I had this gut feeling about not taking the bus, and he said he would drive me. The strange thing was that I only thought about it for one quick second and not anymore. I have since done a lot of research with Maggie here and learned so much that I'll begin listening to my intuition from now on."

Turning to Maggie, Pete asked, "And you, Maggie, you said you had a strange feeling while in the shower. What did it feel like to you?"

Finishing the food she had in her mouth, Maggie answered, "I don't remember too much about that morning. All I remember is that I was washing my hair and I felt really weird. That's when this feeling came over me about asking my mom to drive me and sensing that I shouldn't take the bus. Even now, looking back, I have a hard time explaining exactly what I felt. All I know is that, for some reason, I thought it best not to take the bus. Unlike Gabe, the feeling stuck with me while I showered and got dressed and ready, so I decided I'd better ask for a ride."

"Were you scared when you had the dream about being on the bus?" asked Susan.

"Not really *scared*. I just realized when I woke up what could or would have happened to me if I 'd been on the bus, that I could have been seriously hurt and had a metal rod in my leg. Like Gabe, I've learned to start listening to my intuition more. I had gotten those kinds of feelings in the past but nothing as serious as this one. Like Gabe said, we both learned so much about intuition and psychic abilities doing all that research for the presentation. What I found most interesting was that we all are intuitive and can develop our psychic abilities if we just start paying more attention to them," Maggie said.

By this time at least 10-12 kids were standing around the table listening to what Gabe and Maggie were saying. One of them, Josh, even mentioned his own gut feelings. "I get them a lot and sometimes I listen and other times I just brush them off. After what you both went through and shared yesterday, I'll tell you, I'll definitely pay more attention to them. In fact, I plan on getting a small notebook this afternoon so I can start writing them down as I get them. I think that might be good to begin learning more about intuition and to pay more attention to them."

Before anyone knew it, lunch period was over and the bell rang for everyone to head to their afternoon classes.

As he got up from the table Gabe said, "We have to take our bus home this afternoon, but we'll be around the day after tomorrow before class if you or anyone you know has any more questions."

* * *

With that, everyone headed out of the cafeteria to their classes.

* * *

As the bell ending the last class of the day rang, Gabe headed out to catch the bus. On his way, one of his classmates, Frank, stopped him in the hallway.

"I need to talk to you for a minute about your presentation," Frank said. "I keep having this feeling and dreams about playing football. The problem is, I don't think I'm good enough to play, so I don't even want to try out. I don't want to get embarrassed in front of the other kids. What can I do to get over this?" Frank asked.

Paying close attention to what Frank was saying, Gabe thought for a minute. "I have a few questions. How long have you had these feelings and dreams and why don't you think you are good enough?" Looking around to make sure no one else was listening, Frank continued, "Look at me, I'm not a big, muscular guy. I love football and want to play, but I'm just scared to try out. I've been having these feelings on and off for a long time now. I play in my yard all the time with one of my neighbors. I do everything an offensive end would do. Because of my build and speed, I think I could do it, but I'm afraid."

"Listen, if you have had these feelings for a long time, I think you might want to really sit back and think about them. They're telling you something. It is important to listen to those feelings, but it is also important to believe in yourself. You have to be positive about being able to make the team and stop worrying about not making it. It's like taking a test at school. You know you're going to pass because you believe you will. Well, trying out for the football team is the same thing. You just have to believe you can do it and you will. I bet that deep down, you know you *are* good enough. You just have to bring that forward and keep saying to yourself that you are good enough and you will make the team," concluded Gabe.

Smiling, Frank said, "Thanks, Gabe. I knew you would have the right words for me. I'll definitely follow your advice. Thanks again. Please keep this between us, OK?"

"Sure," said Gabe. "I have to run now, or I'll miss my bus. You keep practicing with your neighbor and believe you can do it."

Gabe saw Maggie saying goodbye to one of her friends as he headed out the door.

She waved at him and walked over to him, "You'll never believe the question Linda just asked me.," she began. "She wanted to about what your gut feeling felt like. I told her that it was just a calm feeling telling you not to take the bus.

Then she told me about the feelings she has had. She said that sometimes when she has had gut feelings, her stomach would hurt a little, and at other times she felt a sense of excitement. She wondered if that was normal or was, she just being a little weird."

"Wow! What did you tell her?" Gabe asked.

"I told her that from all the research you and I did, that gut feelings and intuition can come to people in many different ways. and that sometimes a person could have a little pain, or feel excited, or even relaxed. I said these feelings come to different people in different ways. I also told her that it might help her if she got a journal and wrote down her thoughts and feelings, that she would get more clarity that way," replied Maggie.

As they stepped onto the bus and found their regular seats, Gabe turned and said, "I had a strange talk with Frank right after class." Gabe went on to tell Maggie all about his talk with Frank.

"Have you noticed how things have changed how we're not being teased anymore and how some of the kids are now asking us some serious questions? I think it's great. I think we really did make a good impression and got many of the kids thinking about their feelings and intuition," continued Maggie.

"Yeah, I totally agree," he replied. Gabe was surprised by all of this. "Since there's no school tomorrow because of a teacher workday, and I have very little homework, how about we get together and do a little more research about intuition? I have a feeling we're going to get a lot more questions, that this isn't the end of it."

"Sounds like a great idea. Do you want to come over to my house or for me to go to yours?" asked Maggie, smiling.

"Why don't I come over to your place, say around 10-10:30 in the morning?" Gabe suggested.

"Sure, I'll even make sure my mom has something we can have for lunch. I know she has to work tomorrow, but maybe she can make something ahead of time for us. How does that sound?" asked Maggie.

"I can handle that," he said laughing. "You know me and food."

CHAPTER IX

'T'hat night was quiet at Maggie's house. After she asked her mom if she would whip up something for her and Gabe for lunch tomorrow, explaining what was going on.

"No problem, sweetheart. There's plenty in the fridge. I'll get everything set so all you have to do is heat it up whenever you kids get hungry," said her mom.

With that, Maggie went up to her room to make sure it was clean when Gabe came over and then she lay back on her bed and watched her favorite TV shows. She kept zoning out and daydreaming of Gabe. She liked him so much and felt both a little nervous and excited about spending more time together outside of school and bus trips. She went to sleep that night with a vision of his face in her thoughts.

* * *

Gabe went up to his room after dinner and opened his computer to do more research on intuition. The first thing that popped up was an article about 15 signs that someone is a deeply intuitive person. The more he read, the more interested he became. He started making all kinds of notes to show Maggie. He read with fascination as each sign seemed even more amazing than the previous one. *I wonder if anyone at school has this ability,* one thought. He continued reading well into the night. He found other interesting articles including one about Indigo children, which he printed to take to Maggie's. He decided to work mainly on the article about the 15 signs of being a deeply intuitive person.

Before he realized it, it was almost midnight. He shut down his computer and jumped into bed. He was so tired from all the reading that he fell asleep as soon as his head hit the pillow.

Since there was no school the next day, he hadn't set his alarm. As he rolled over, he looked at the clock and saw that it was almost 8:30. Panicking a little, he jumped out of bed and headed to the bathroom to get cleaned up and dressed. He had told Maggie he would be there around 10, and he wanted to show her that he could keep his word. He downed his breakfast in record time and went back to his room to get his computer and notes to bring to Maggie's. *Wait until Maggie sees what I found,* he thought. That made him even more excited to see her as if he really needed a reason for that. He grinned as he thought of her almost the entire way to her house.

* * *

At exactly 10 am, Gabe rang Maggie's doorbell. When she opened the door, she immediately noticed the excited look on his face. She wondered if his expression had to do with him being with her or something else.

Gabe blurted out, "Wait until I show you what I found last night! It will blow your mind, Maggie, just like it did mine. I can't wait to show you."

"Wow, it must be something really big for you to be so excited. I've never seen you this excited except the night we kissed," replied Maggie.

Still smiling, he said, "Well, yeah. That was totally amazing, and I loved it, but this is totally different."

"OK then, let's head into the dining room. I made room for us there since my mom and dad aren't home today. We're alone," replied Maggie as she led Gabe to the dining room.

* * *

Just as they got to the table, Maggie's phone rang. "Oh, it's my friend Cindy. I'd better see wants she wants."

"Hi Cindy, what's up?" asked Maggie, answering the phone. "Yeah, you can come over. I need to tell you that Gabe is here so whatever you have to say, do you mind saying it in front of him?"

"No," Cindy replied. "In fact, I think he might want to hear this too. I didn't want to talk about it at school because I didn't know how the other kids would react. So, if you don't mind, I'll hop in the car and head on over."

"Come on over. We aren't going anywhere. Going to do a little more research on the subject of intuition," replied Maggie.

Smiling a little, Cindy said, "That's perfect because what I want to talk about has to do with just that. I'm leaving now. See you in about 15 minutes."

Turning to Gabe, Maggie said, "Now, that was interesting. Did you hear any of our conversation?"

"Sorry, no. I wasn't paying any attention," said Gabe.

"Well, it seems Cindy wants to talk to us about intuition and psychic abilities and doesn't want to talk about it at school because she doesn't know how the other kids will react." Maggie felt a little puzzled by Cindy's reluctance to discuss it at school.

"Now that is interesting to hear. When is she coming over?" asked Gabe.

"She's on her way over now. Should be here in about 15 minutes. So do you want to tell me what you are so excited about? What did you find?"

"Why don't we wait until Cindy gets here," Gabe replied. "I want to hear what she wants to talk about. Besides, what I found will take longer than 15 minutes to explain."

In what seemed like no time at all, Maggie's doorbell rang. It startled both of them. Maggie jumped up to answer it, while Gabe stayed in the dining room.

"Hi, Cindy. Boy, that was fast. We didn't expect you for another five or so minutes," said Maggie as she opened the door.

"There was very little traffic all the way over. Oh, is it OK to park in your driveway for a while?" asked Cindy.

Looking toward the driveway, Maggie replied, "Sure, it's OK, as long as it's moved before my folks get home around 5 to 5:30."

"No problem. I hope what I have to say and ask doesn't take that long," answered Cindy.

Showing Cindy into the dining room, Maggie said, "Great. Then we have almost all day to discuss what's on your mind. I hope we can help. I think you know Gabe already."

Nodding at Gabe, "Yes, we never actually met, but I've seen him around school and lately with you. Hi Gabe. I enjoyed your presentation the other day. And yours too Maggie. Intuition is a subject that's been on my mind for a long time. I think it goes back to when I was in the eighth grade. At least that's as far back as I can remember."

Standing up and pulling out a chair for Cindy to sit, Gabe said, "Nice meeting you too, and thank you for the compliment on our presentation. So, what's been bothering you that you don't feel like you can ask us or talk about at school?"

Looking a little worried, Cindy started. "Like I said, going back as far as the eighth grade, I've been able to sense and understand what others are feeling even before they say anything. Sometimes it's so strong I can feel the pain or joy they are feeling before they tell me about it. During the presentation, you talked about psychic abilities. It got me thinking and wondering if that's what I've been experiencing all these years. And that's only part of it. I can meet someone for the first time, and after a minute or two, I can tell if they're for real or if they're hiding something. So you can see why I didn't want to talk to you guys at school. I don't want others to think I'm some kind of freak who they don't want to be around. I couldn't handle that."

Looking directly at Cindy, Maggie said, "Yeah, I can see why you wouldn't want to say anything with other kids around. I'd say you definitely have psychic ability. What do you think, Gabe?"

"The two of you won't believe this, but what Cindy is talking about is exactly what I was so excited about when I came over this morning. This has to do with the research I found last night. The article talked about 15 signs that indicate a person is a deeply intuitive individual. Cindy, it seems you are an example of exactly that. Would you two mind if I went on and talked about everything I found out last night? Cindy, I'd like to know how many of these signs relate to you." "Sure," said Cindy nodding.

Maggie was excited to hear the information too. She said, "Go ahead, Gabe. This sounds really interesting."

Gabe began., "Well, the first two signs they talk about are exactly what you say you experience, Cindy. They call it a strong sense of empathy and a sixth sense. What you described about yourself is almost identical to what the article stated. The third sign it mentioned was being a dreamer. The article says that intuitive people have a rich inner world and a vivid imagination that shows up in their dreams. You may have dreams that feel real and sometimes leave a lasting impression on you, similar to the one Maggie had about actually being on the bus when it crashed. Next, it talked about being curious, asking 'why' and 'how', and wanting to learn as much as you can. What I do know about you, Cindy, is that you're a good listener. You actually sit and listen to what others have to say. It seems to me that you don't listen just to answer them but to understand them.

Gabe continued, "Highly intuitive people have a heightened sensitivity to their surroundings and can sense the energy in a room when it changes. They know when energy is positive or negative.

They also have a strong intuition about people. They have a strong sense of whether or not to trust someone. Highly intuitive people have a strong connection with their bodies. They know when something is off with their bodies. The article says there are also those who are natural healers. They can sense when someone needs healing even if the person doesn't say anything. They don't necessarily heal the person, but they offer comfort and support to those in need. Decision-making can and normally is very tough, but intuitive people often have a natural ability to lead and make decisions. It's because they are attuned to their own needs and the needs of those around them. They have a sense of what is best for themselves and those around them and have the confidence to make things happen. If all that isn't enough, highly intuitive people have a strong connection to nature. It's because they're attuned to the energy and vibrations of the world around them. The twelfth sign is that they are deep thinkers and have a strong sense of purpose. They have a deep understanding of the world around them and are attuned to their own passions and desires. They possess a strong spiritual connection that can manifest as a deep connection to a higher power or a belief in something greater than themselves. They tend to be natural teachers or mentors too. That goes back to helping and supporting others. Finally, the fifteenth sign is that they have a strong sense of justice but are also natural peacemakers. They have a deep sense of fairness and are always seeking to create balance and harmony. The article says they have a strong desire to make a positive impact on the world."

Maggie was in awe listening to the information. Her attention remained fixed on Gabe as he continued.

Gabe continued, "What I also found was an article about indigo children that listed their common traits. Let me read that. First, they are empathic and strong-willed and are often perceived as shy or as being strange by friends and family. They have a clear sense of self-definition and purpose, show a strong innate subconscious spirituality from early childhood, and have a strong feeling of entitlement or deserving to be here. They're also highly intelligent, have an inherent intuitive ability, and. are resistant to rigid, control-based paradigms of authority.' The article explained each of these traits, which I found very interesting. Now you can see why I was so excited to tell you about all this. So, Cindy, do any of these signs or traits resonate with you?"

Maggie gazed intently at her friend, anxious to hear her reply.

"Are you kidding me? I don't relate to *all* the signs and traits, but a lot of them describe me to a T. If you don't mind, I'd like a copy of those articles. I guess I really have psychic abilities even more than I ever thought. I was so worried there was something really wrong with me. Thanks to you, I now know that I have abilities far beyond what I thought. You have no idea how much I appreciate what you just said. Thank you very much," said Cindy.

Beaming with excitement, Maggie commented, "Unreal, totally unreal! Now I see why you've been so excited to talk about this. I bet there are many people who have these abilities but are afraid to talk about them or even face them. I wonder if they even know who to talk to about them. Can you imagine what the average kid would say if someone, even briefly, mentioned any of these signs or traits and the fact that they had many of them? Cindy, I completely understand why you didn't want to talk about any of this at school. There's no doubt that many of the kids would call you all kinds of names and think you were a freak, but you're not. There's so much more for us to learn about intuition, gut feelings, psychic abilities, and indigo children. We could go on for hours and days and I bet we wouldn't even begin to scratch the surface. Thank you both for bringing this up today. What makes it even more interesting is the fact, that we know someone who has many of these abilities and traits. Also, I think Gabe was led by his own intuition to find these articles."

"A crazy thought just came to me," said Gabe. "I wonder if Mr. Preston would allow us to write an article for the school paper on this subject so others who might have these abilities and are afraid to talk about them would understand themselves and their abilities better."

"I bet he would," said Cindy. "Please, just don't mention my name. I'm not ready to let everyone know about my ability."

Nodding her head, Maggie replied, "I think he would too. It would be worth a try. We can tell him what you found, Gabe, and let him know that one of the kids from school talked to us and that they have these abilities and traits and were worried that something was wrong with them. We can add that the person thought it was a negative thing and not a gift. I say we go for it. And, Cindy, don't worry, we won't mention your name. We'll just say 'someone.' We won't even say if it was a boy or a girl, just that someone came and talked to us."

* * *

The three of them agreed with the plan. They spent the rest of the day writing and editing an article to present to Mr. Preston the next day.

"I can't believe we've been at this all afternoon. It's almost dinner time," said Cindy after looking at her phone.

At that moment, Maggie's mom walked through the front door. "Are you kids still at it?" she asked.

Surprised at the time and hearing her mom, Maggie replied, "Yeah, Mom. We've been working on an article we're going to present to Mr. Preston for the school paper."

"That sounds great, but I think Gabe and Cindy need to head home for dinner," her mom replied.

Maggie could hardly believe how fast the day had flown by.

Gabe and Cindy were already gathering their paperwork and computers.

"It was a great afternoon, Maggie," Cindy said. "Thanks so much. I'll see you at school in the morning," Cindy, finished loading her backpack and headed for the door.

"Wait for me," Gabe said. "Cindy, can you give me a lift home?"

"Sure," smiled Cindy.

Turning to Maggie's mom, Gabe, and Cindy said their goodbyes and headed for the door.

Maggie escorted them to the door and said, "Gabe, see you on the bus tomorrow morning. And, Cindy, thanks so much for feeling comfortable enough to talk to Gabe and me. See you at school, and I promise we won't say anything, "Maggie felt a little overwhelmed ball the information from Gabe's research and the revelations from Cindy about her intuitive abilities. She decided not to share anything about that with her family. She just wanted to relax, have dinner, and zone out in front of the TV.

As Maggie was watching her favorite sitcom, her phone rang. It was Gabe.

"Hey there, I didn't expect to hear from you tonight," Maggie said after she picked up the phone.

"I still cannot believe how today worked out, with Cindy coming over and me having the articles that were so much in line with what Cindy talked about. Unreal," said Gabe.

"I know. I was thinking about the same thing a little while ago. I guess that is our intuition working in sync," she said with a smile.

Almost laughing, Gabe commented, "Yeah, you could say that, couldn't you? Anyway, I'll let you get back to whatever you were doing and see you in the morning. Have a good night's sleep."

"You too," replied Maggie as she hung up the phone.

* * *

"Morning, Gabe," said Maggie as Gabe stepped onto the bus. "Did you bring the article with you and is it ready to give to Mr. Preston?"

"Yes and yes," said Gabe. "It is all typed and ready to hand to him first thing when we get to school. I think we should just tell him what we found and let him read it while we're in class. Then, if he has any questions or comments, he can tell us at lunch."

"Sounds good to me," answered Maggie.

Their friend Rose was there to greet them as they stepped off the bus. "Well, any new gossip I need to hear?"

"No, Rose," Maggie replied. "Gabe and I just did a little more research yesterday on the subject of intuition. We have an article we're presenting to Mr. Preston, and we're hoping, he'll print it in the school paper."

Rose had one of those sly grins on her face, she said, "Sure, I'll just bet that's what the two of you did yesterday."

Pulling the article out of his backpack, Gabe showed it to Rose.

"Sorry about that. I guess you *were* doing research yesterday," said Rose.

The bell rang indicating they needed to get to homeroom. Gabe and Maggie headed to the school office to see Mr. Preston instead.

"If you two will wait a minute I'll see if Mr. Preston can see you," said his secretary.

"Good morning you two," the principal said smiling. I didn't expect to see you two again so soon. Is there a problem?" asked Mr. Preston.

"No, sir," answered Gabe. "Maggie and I did some additional research yesterday and wrote an article about intuition, psychic abilities, and indigo children. We'd like you to read it and hopefully publish it in the next edition of the school paper if you think that's a good idea. We need to get to the cafeteria in case anyone comes with more questions, but, if you have the time and would like to talk to us about it, we can stop by on our way to lunch."

Looking briefly at the article, Mr. Preston replied, "My morning is pretty free, so I'll look it over and if you would please stop by on your way to lunch, I'll let the two of know what I think."

"Thank you, sir," said Maggie as they turned to head to the cafeteria.

* * *

The last bell before lunch sounded and both Maggie and Gabe headed back to Mr. Preston's office.

As they entered the outer office, they saw Mr. Preston waiting for them. "I read over your article and I'm very impressed with what you wrote. I personally know a couple of people who have the abilities you have written about. I'll be more than happy to publish it in next week's school paper. It is too late to get into this edition. You both continually amaze me. Great work! By the way, was there someone in school who has these abilities or traits?"

"Yes, but we promised not to say who it is because the person is afraid, they will be teased and bullied," said Maggie.

Nodding, Mr. Preston replied, "I totally understand. I don't want to know who it is. Please tell them I understand."

"Will do," said Maggie.

As the days went by, everything seemed to be back to normal. Classmates continued to ask Gabe and Maggie once in a while, but things were much calmer and nothing like those first few days after the presentation.

Gabe was just happy to spend more time with Maggie as their relationship grew closer every day. He called her each night via video chat, and they held hands on the bus to and from school.

The following week, they talked at length on the night before the newspaper was published.

"Well, tomorrow is the day the article comes out," Gabe said. "Are you at all nervous and wondering how everyone will react?'

"Yeah, I am." She replied. He could see her brow furrow slightly as it did every time she was worried or concerned. She had the tiniest intention between her eyebrows from that look. "I just keep wondering if our names will be published with the article or will it just be the article. Not sure if I want to see our names with it," replied Maggie.

"I know. I wish we would have told Mr. Preston not to print our names as the authors of the article," he said, questioning his choice not to ask that their names be withheld. "But it's too late now. All we can do is hope for the best. This past week and a half has really been great. I mean we have had some questions, but mainly things have gotten back to nor-

mal. I wonder if this article will stir it all up again." As she said the words, a feeling of unease rose in his chest.

"It might, but you have to remember," Maggie said, "we chose to do this, and we're helping Cindy even though no one knows who it is," answered Maggie. "At least tomorrow is Friday, and we only have to deal with it for one day before the weekend."

She always seemed to say the right thing to ease his mind. Gabe thought. She smiled at him as if somehow, she had read his thoughts.

Maggie added, "It's getting late and I want to get a good night's sleep. See you on the bus tomorrow!" She blew him a kiss through the phone.

"Good night to you too. Pleasant dreams," he said as he blew a kiss to her return. After he hung up the video call illiam McDonald

and turned off his phone, he lay there for a while just remembering their actual kiss. That hadn't happened again since, but he knew when the time was right it would.

* * *

"Well, today's the day," said Maggie as Gabe took his normal seat next to her.

"Yeah, here goes nothing. I'm beginning to think everything will go just fine," Gabe said.

As they exited the bus at school, they saw Rose running up to them with a school newspaper in her hand. "You two are the hit of the school. Kids all over are talking about the article you published. I haven't heard one negative remark either. Everyone loves it! I even heard a couple of the kids saying they could relate to a couple of the signs and traits you wrote about. What really got to me was that I heard one of the boys talking to his friends about his abilities. He said he was always afraid to say anything for fear he would get teased, but your article made him feel more relaxed to talk about it. I wasn't able to hear everything he said, but it sounded like he really has many of the signs of being a psychic that you mentioned."

Looking at the article, Maggie could see that her and Gabe's names were listed as the authors.

"Are you kidding me?" asked Gabe. "I guess everything is going to be OK today. Maggie and I were a little worried about how everyone would take the article. I guess we don't have to worry anymore, do we, Maggie?"

Before she could even respond, a group of kids came running up to them thanking them for opening up and not hiding things about intuition and psychic abilities.

"This article is great," one of the girls said. "It's even better than the presentation you two gave a couple of weeks ago. I've been having dreams sometimes about things that I didn't understand. Now I'm going to write them down and see what they are all about. Thank you. You two have no idea what this article's done for so many of us. I know that some of my closest friends have been talking to me in private about how their intuition has been raised since the presentation and how they've done more research on the subject."

Before Maggie or Gabe could respond, the bell rang for homeroom.

"See you at lunch," yelled Gabe, as he entered the front of the school.

Maggie was inundated with questions and comments all morning and imagined that Gabe was too. A couple of girls even told her they related to many of the signs in the article.

Maggie caught up with Gabe just outside the cafeteria. She spotted his green shirt that always brought out the depths of his brown eyes. Once she was in earshot, she started telling him about all the comments she received during the morning. Gabe just listened. He was always patient with her bout of verbal diarrhea.

"Wow, "Gabe said. "I got lots of feedback too. A couple of guys came up and quietly told me that they believed they had psychic ability one even whispered in my ear that he researched indigo children because friends of his parents said they believed he was an indigo child. He asked me not to mention it to anyone, so I can't tell you who it was, but I thought it was amazing that they were willing to talk to me about their feelings." Gabe added. "What a far cry from the day we gave the original presentation and the day after."

"Yeah, I agree," Maggie replied. "I think the article in today's school paper was a great addition to our presentation about intuition and psychic abilities. You did a great job," she replied.

Smiling, Gabe said, "Thanks but it wasn't all me. You played a major part in all this and so did Cindy sharing her abilities last week. I think it's obvious that our strange feelings on the day of the bus accident were meant to lead us to this point to get the word out to many people and let them know the importance of paying more attention. I also can't believe how many of the kids have these abilities and keep them to themselves. I only hope this helped them to be less afraid to share their abilities and help others."

"You're right. What we did was meant to be. We were being told how important it is to let others know so they wouldn't have to hide any longer. I'm so glad we did all this. Besides, it even got you to open up about how you felt about me," she said, laughing. "Heck, everyone else in the school knew it but you and me."

"There goes the bell. See you after school on the bus," said Gabe.

As Maggie stepped onto the bus, she saw Gabe was already seated, which was unusual. She plopped down beds him, glad to be close to him again. She said, "This afternoon was pretty much like this morning, just more positive comments and a couple of questions."

"Me too," Gabe replied. "So, since all this is finished, what do you want to do this weekend? Would you like to go to a movie with me?"

"Wow, are you asking me out on a date?" she asked. "If so, my answer is yes! There are a couple of movies I've been dying to see. Can I pick the movie, or do you want to?"

"Sure, anyone you want to see is OK with me. I just want to spend some time with you when we're not working on presentations and articles," answered Gabe. "Just let me know what movie you want to see, and I'll check everything out and let you know the times."

As the bus pulled up to Gabe's stop, Maggie said, "OK then, I'll talk to you later."

The bus started again with a jolt forward, and Maggie watched him walk away headed toward his house until the bus rounded a corner and he was out of sight. On the bumpy ride home, she thought back about their strange journey of the last few weeks. Little did she imagine that morning how their lives would change. Now, the entire school knew a lot more about intuition and psychic abilities, and she and Gabe had grown closer in the process of discovering and uncovering the knowledge that might help so many people. She wondered if Gabe would be a part of her life in the years to come.

Would she still have these feelings for him during senior year and beyond.? Just then, an overwhelming feeling rose within her, and a picture entered her mind of Gabe liking looking older and more mature, gazing into her eyes with that expression she had glimpsed a few times since he shared his feelings about her. In an instant, the vision was gone, but the sense it left behind remained. *I think just maybe we'll be close for a long, long time,* she said silently to herself. *Yep, I just have a feeling.* She smiled at the thought as the bus creaked to a stop in front of her house, jerking hie slightly back to the present moment.

AUTHOR'S COMMENTS

The story you just read may sound entirely fictional, but experiences like Gabe's and Maggie's happen every day. Everyone is intuitive, but I know many people who have developed or were born with these psychic abilities. Twenty years ago I met and married a woman who has these abilities. Most mornings she tells me things that were shared with her just before she awakened. She is *never* wrong. Her mother had this gift also. My wife and I have met a few teenagers who have these abilities, both boys and girls, so, don't think it is only a female thing. Authors like me often have strong intuitions as well. I believe that my writing comes from my intuition. The majority of the time I do not even know what I am writing until I stop and read over what I wrote. I've talked to other authors who totally agree with me when it comes to their writing. So, if someone talks to you about something they sensed, don't laugh, and shrug your shoulders. Believe what they are telling you. It may even save your life.

Trust your gut feelings and intuition. You will be glad you did.

Remember, we all are intuitive.

www.ingramcontent.com/pod-product-compliance
Lightning Source LLC
Chambersburg PA
CBHW070704130626
46553CB00005B/1827